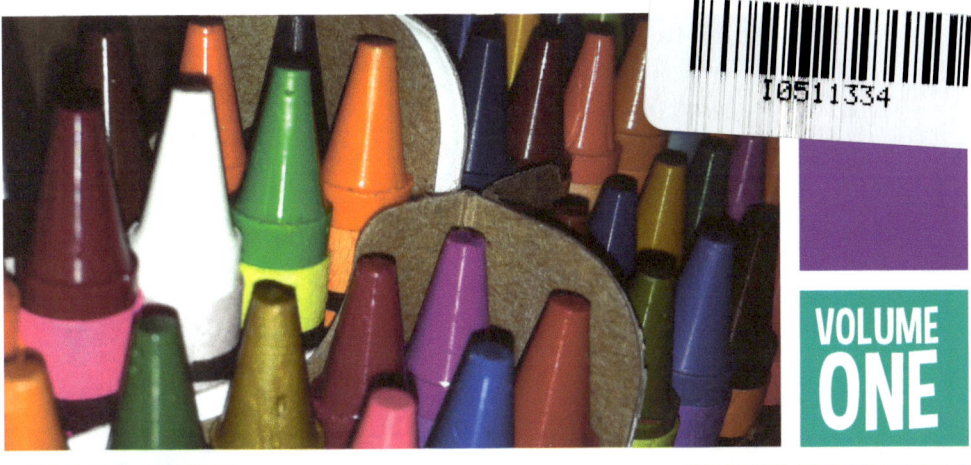

VOLUME ONE

ART BY MARK

Mark Mariano

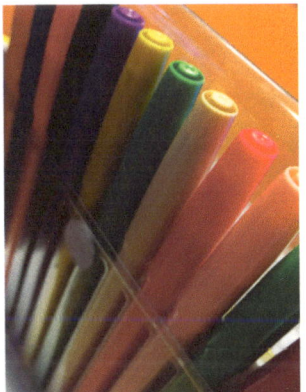

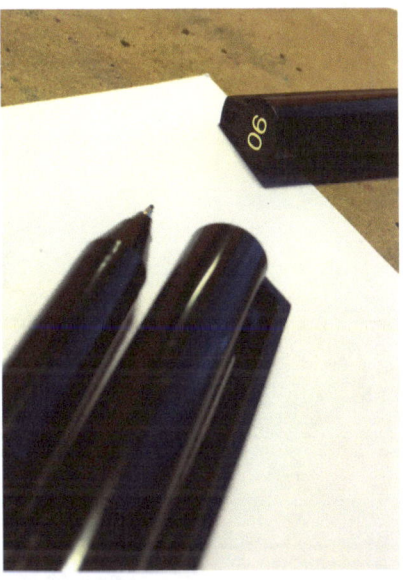

First Edition, September 2015
ISBN 978-1514648551

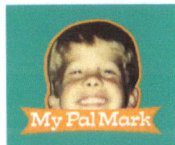

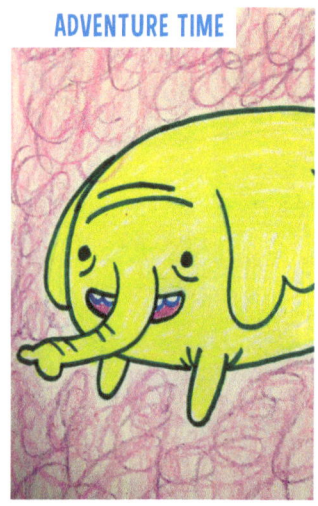
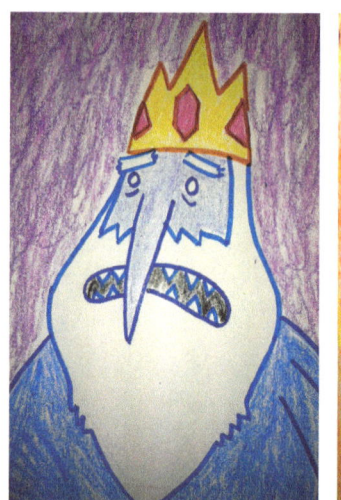
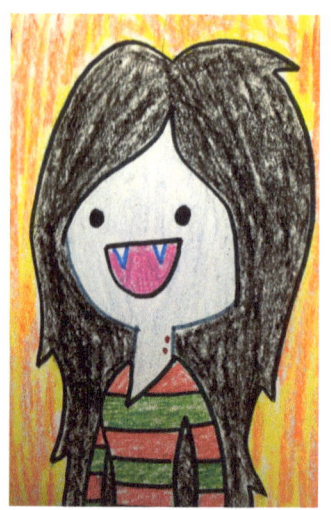
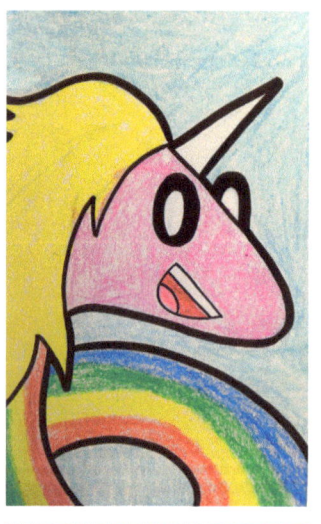
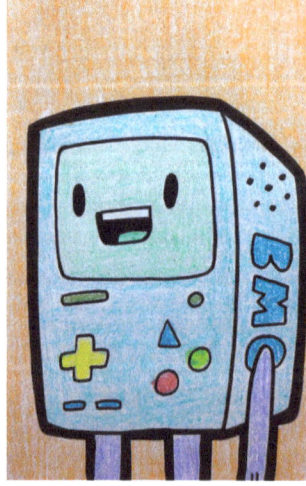
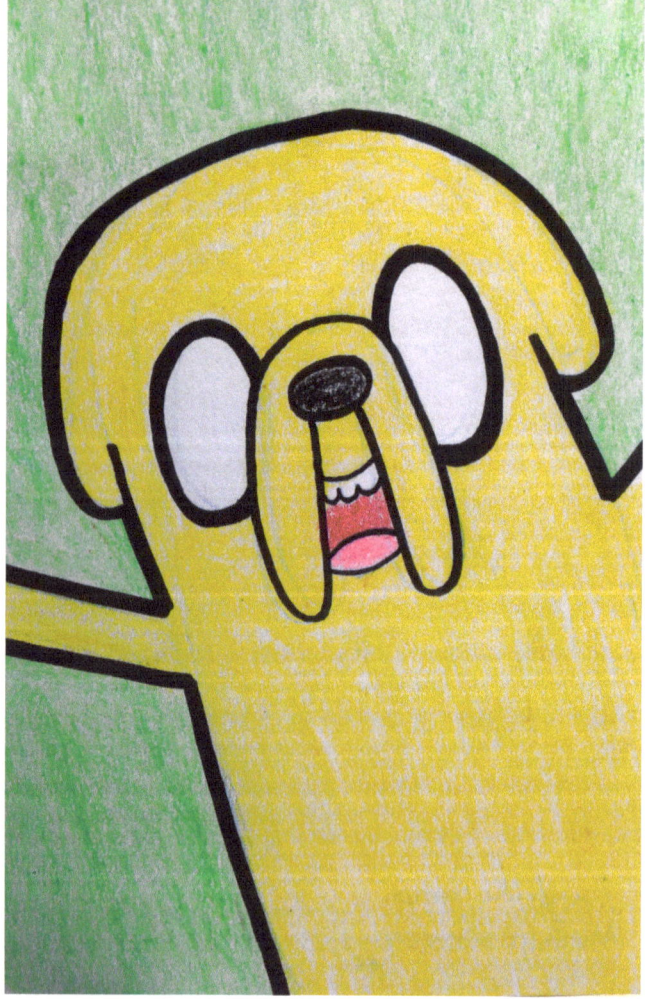

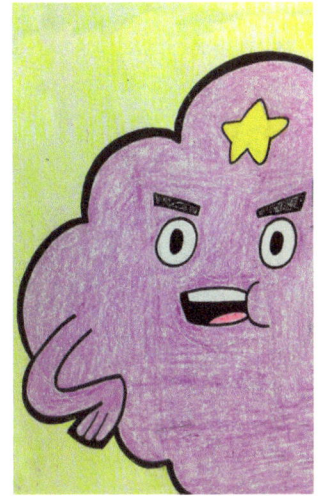
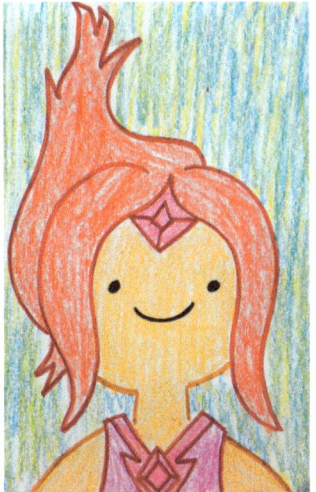
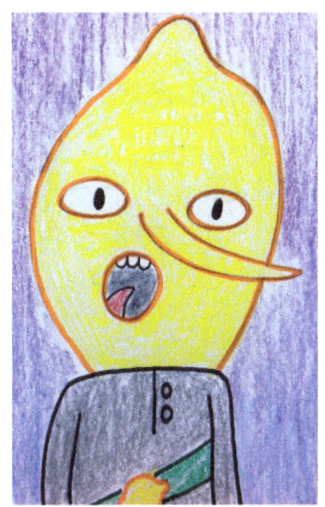
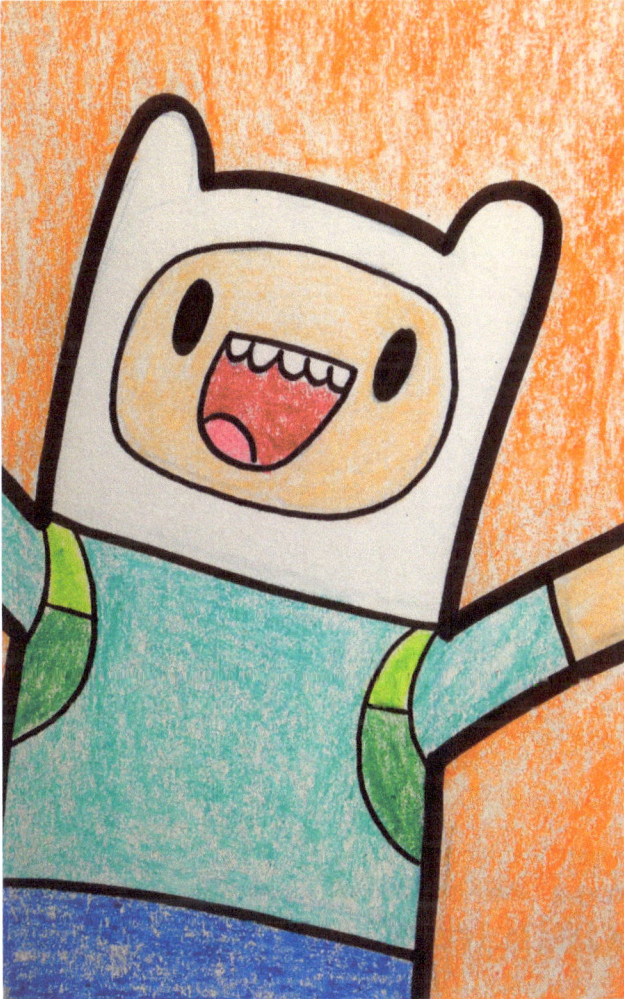
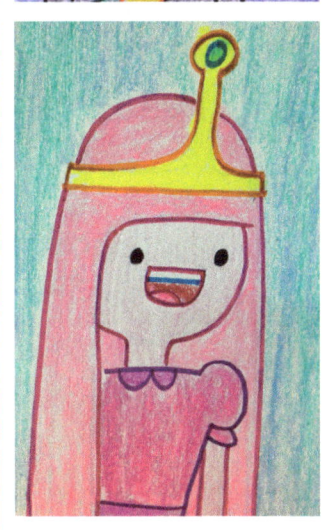

OTHER PAGE:
Tree Trunks, Ice King,
Marceline, Lady Rainicorn,
BMO, Jake

THIS PAGE:
Lumpy Space Princess,
Flame Princess,
Lemongrab, Finn,
Pincess Bubblegum

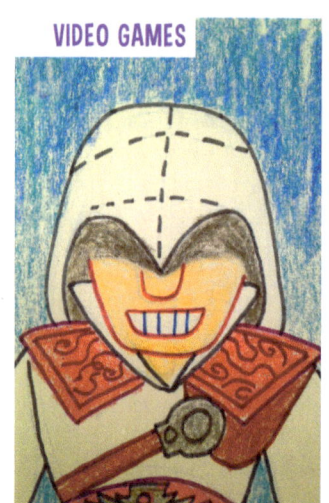

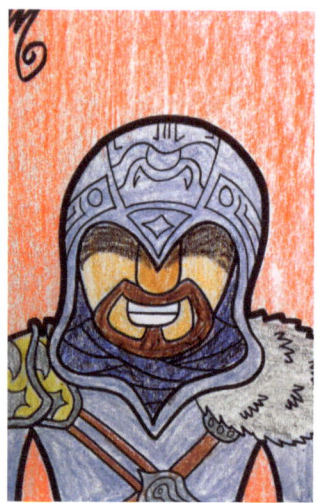

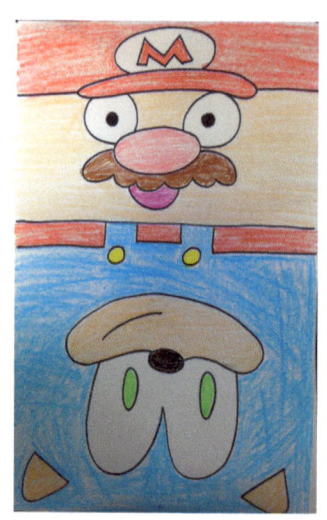

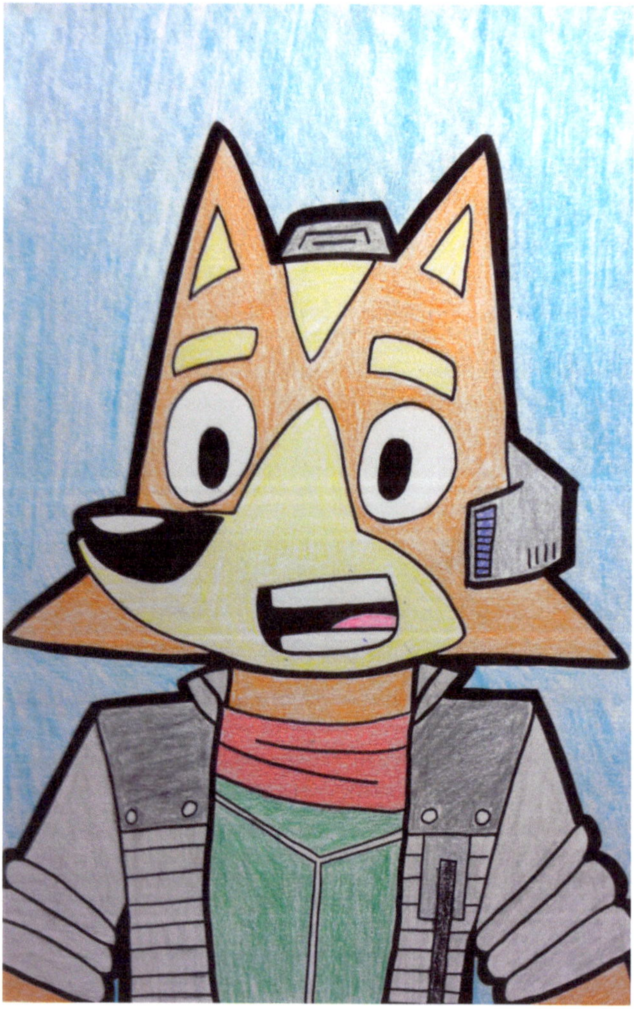

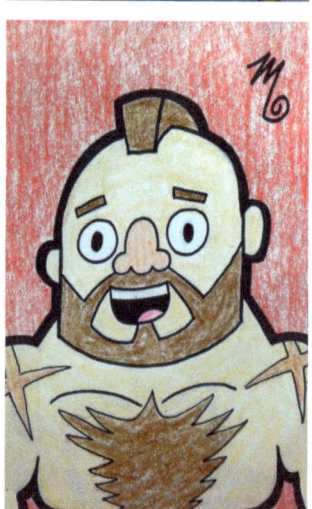

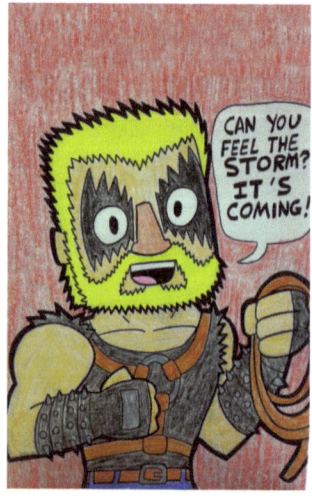

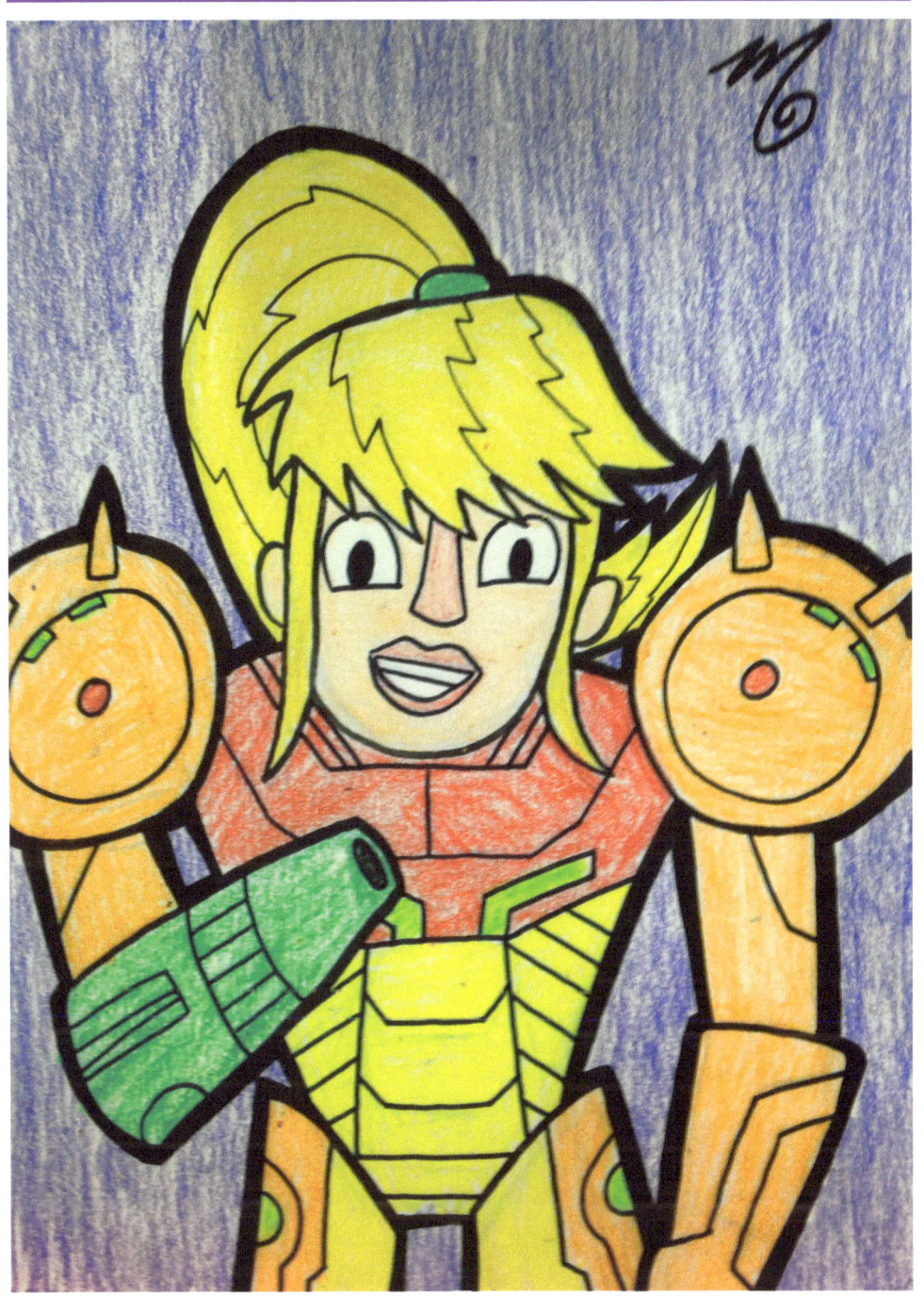

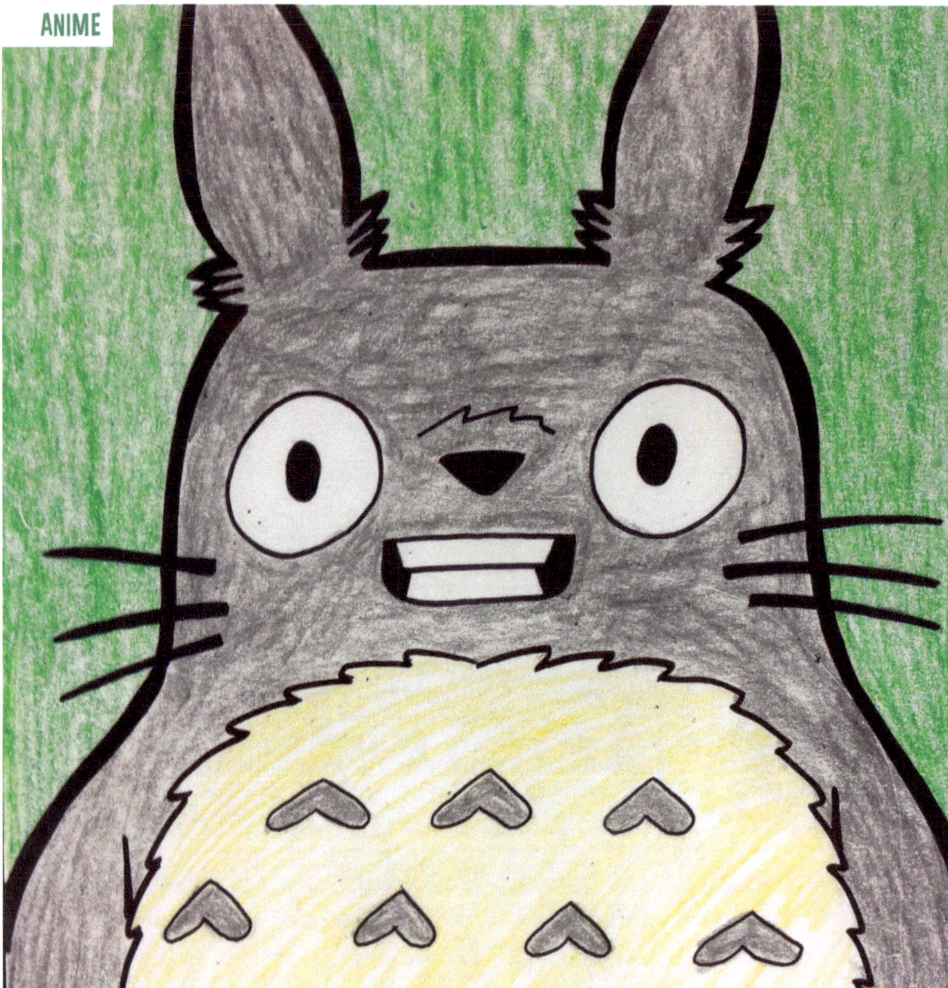

THIS PAGE:
Totoro
Nausicaa
Kodama

OTHER PAGE:
Toonami Tom
Usopp
Kimba
Black Butler

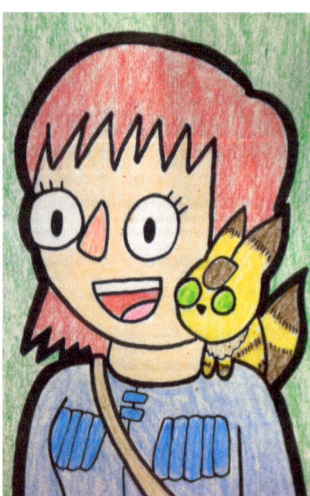

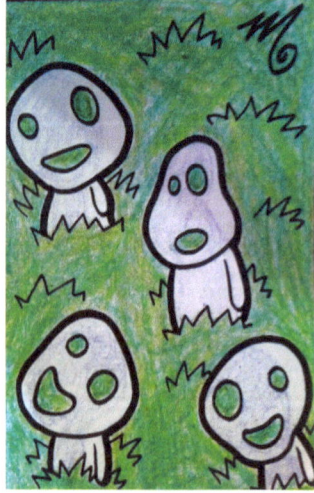

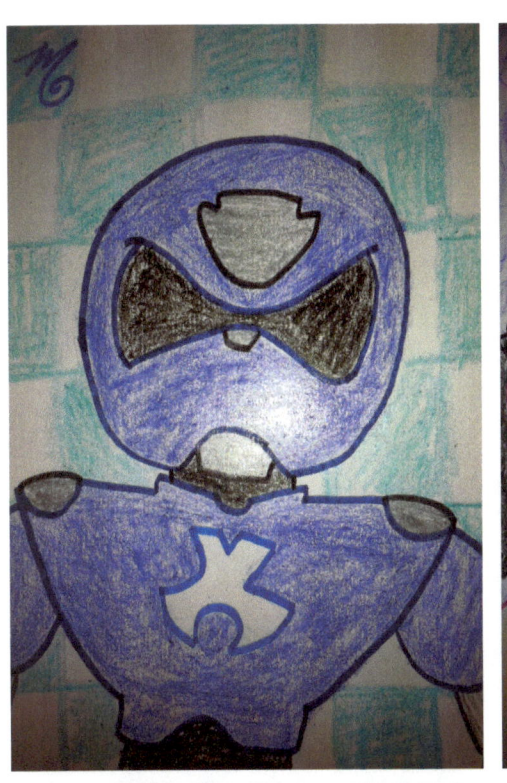
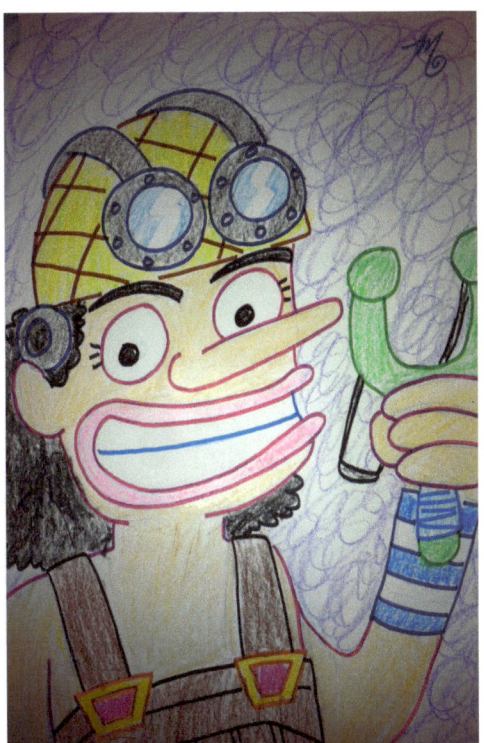
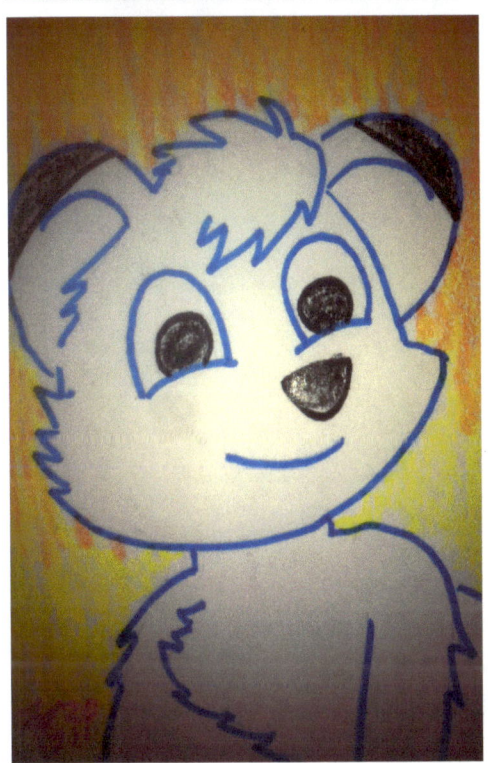
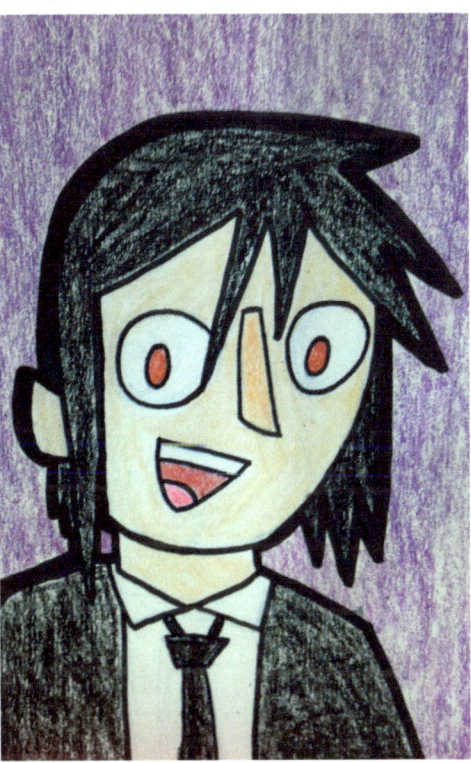

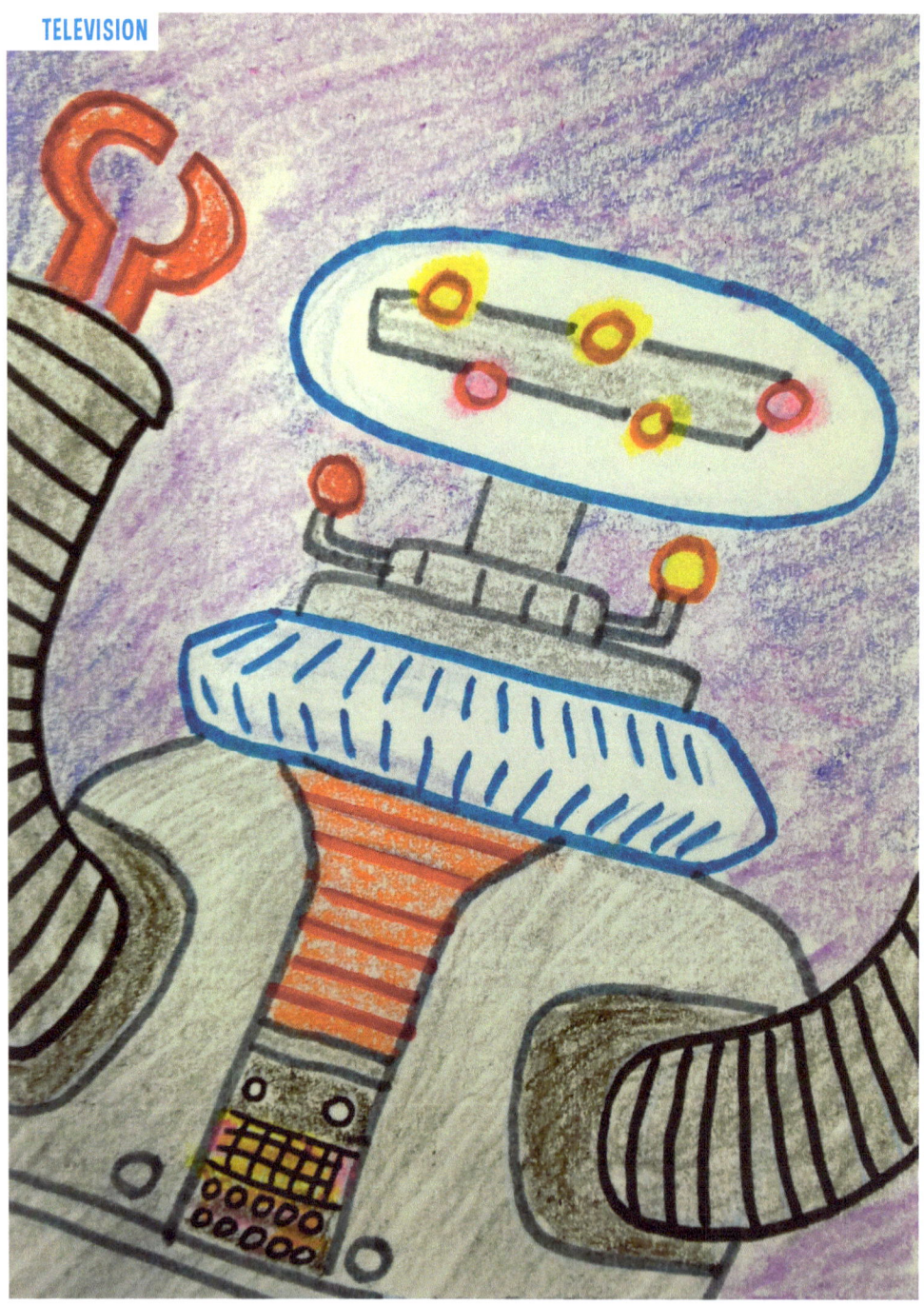

THIS PAGE: B-9 Robot

OTHER PAGE: Alf, Mork, Red Ranger, White Ranger, Green Ranger

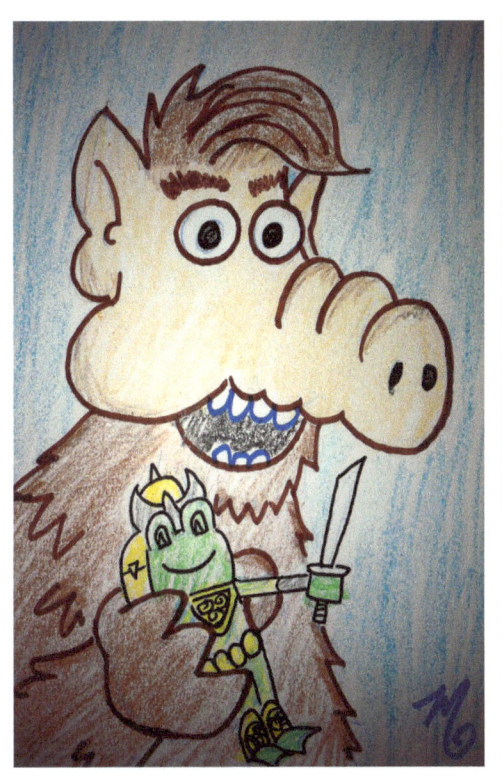

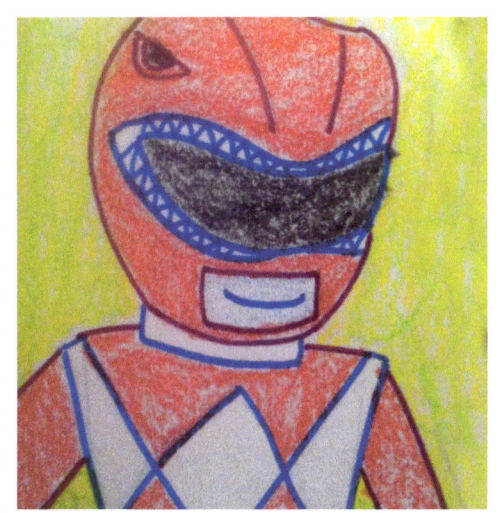

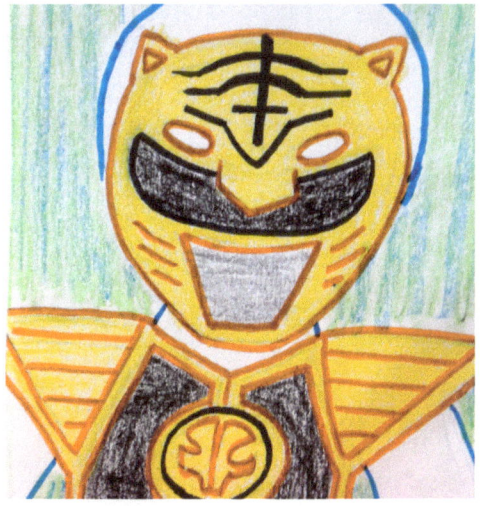

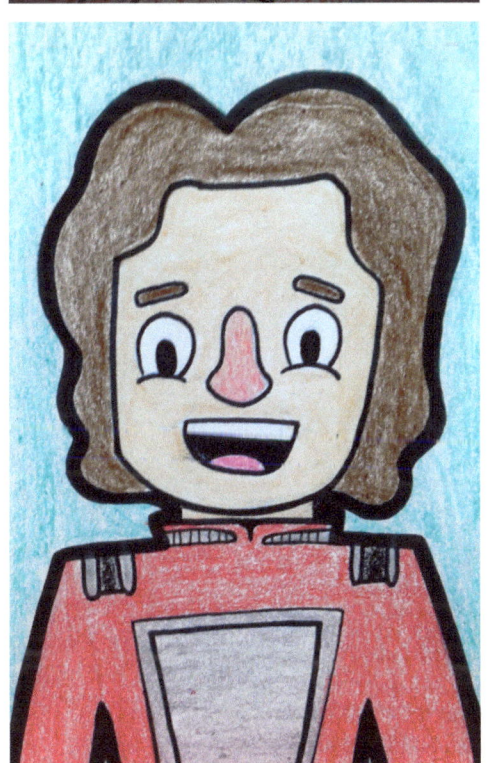

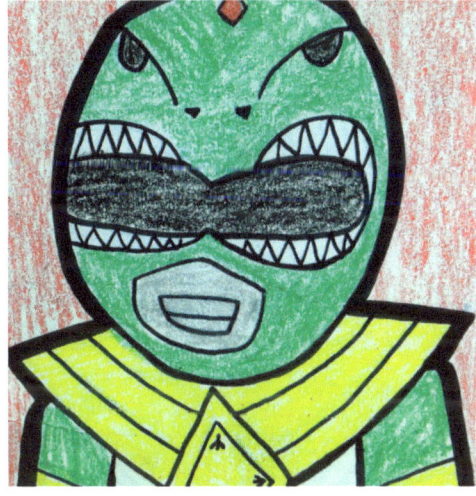

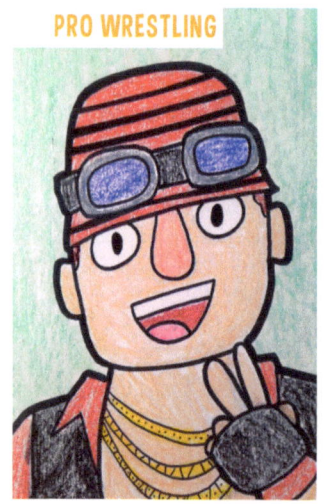
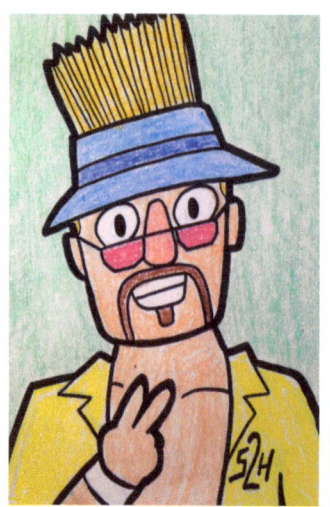
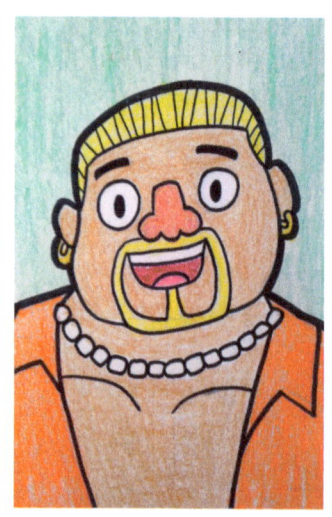
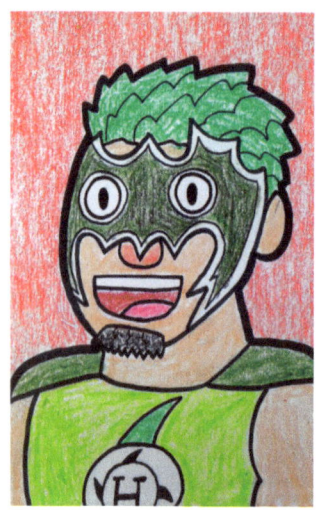
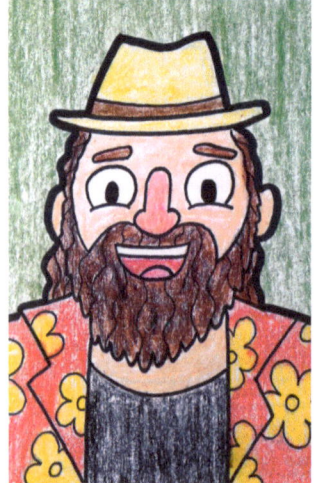
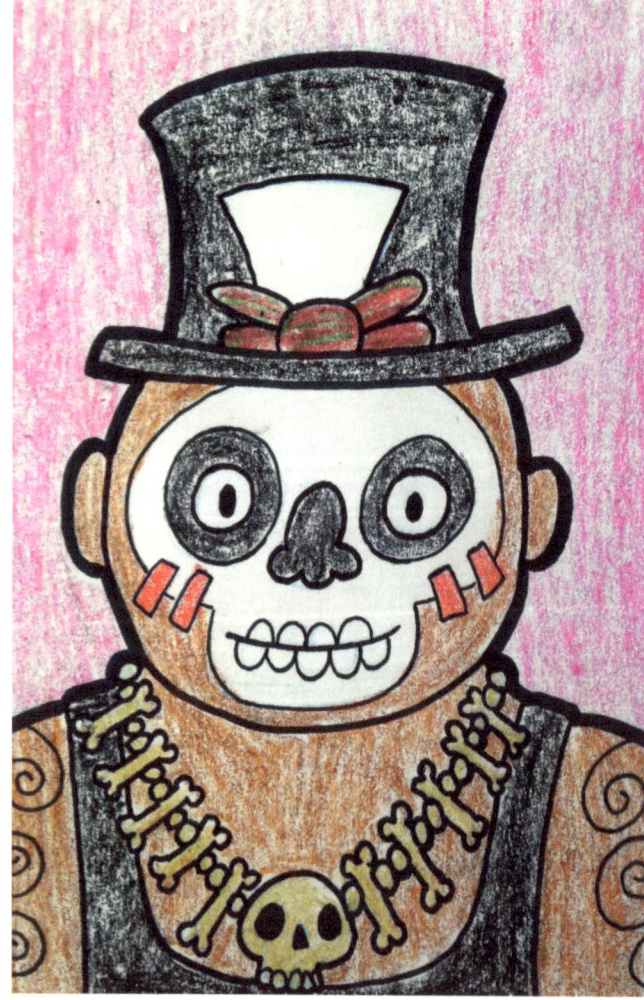

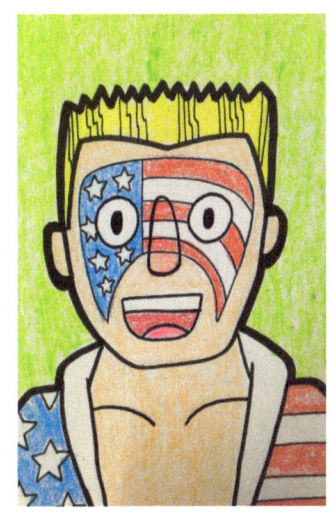
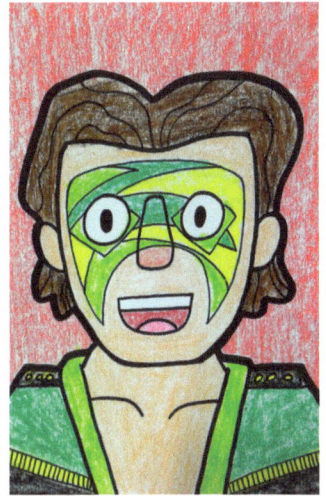
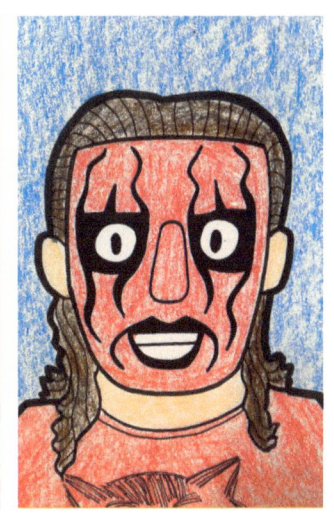
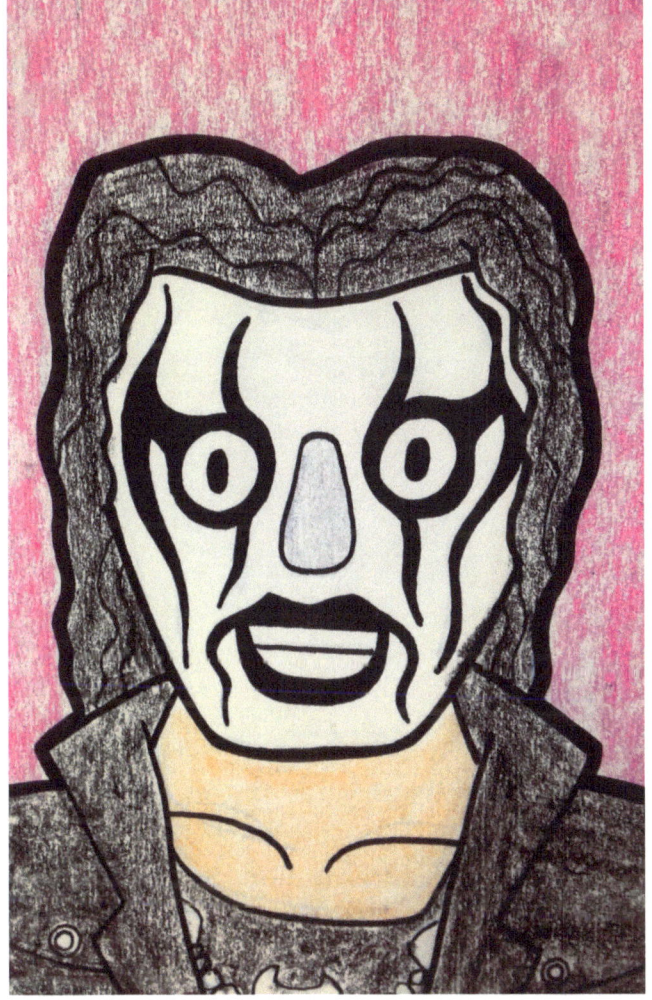
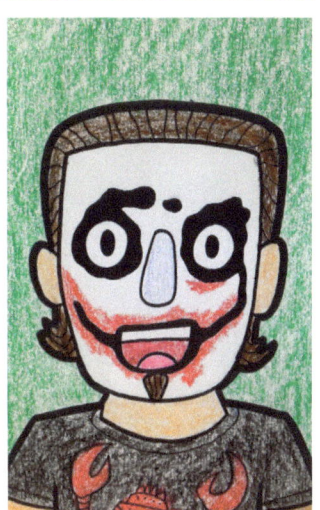

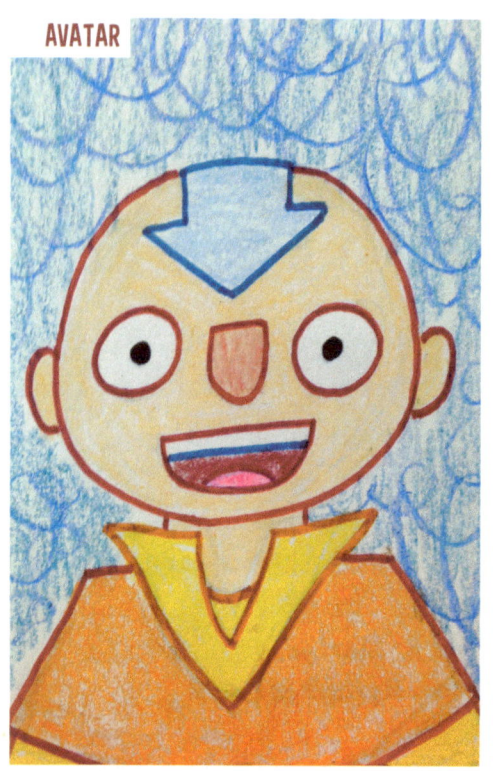
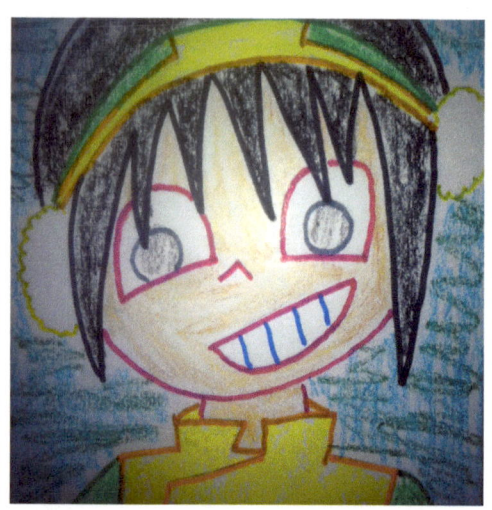
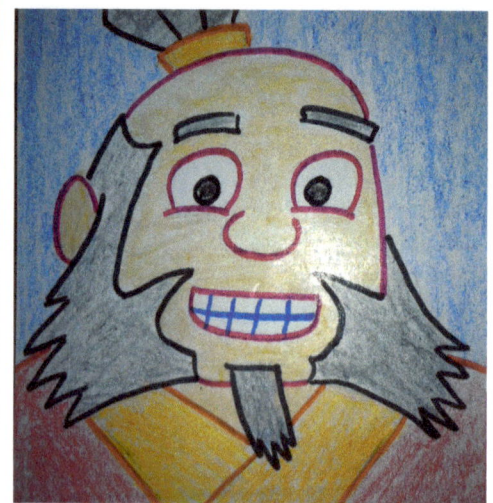
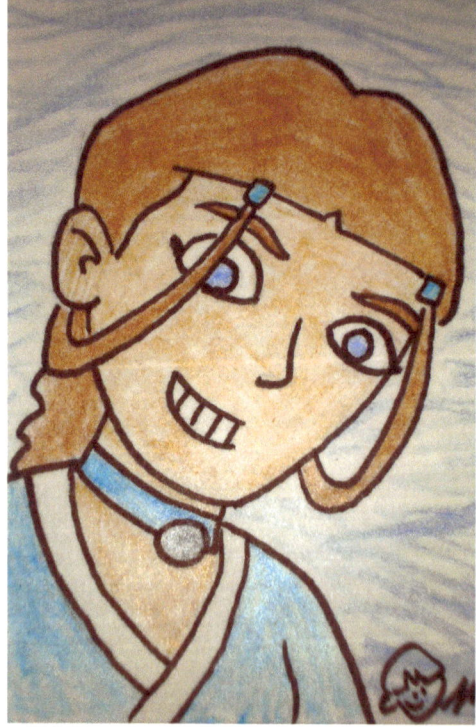
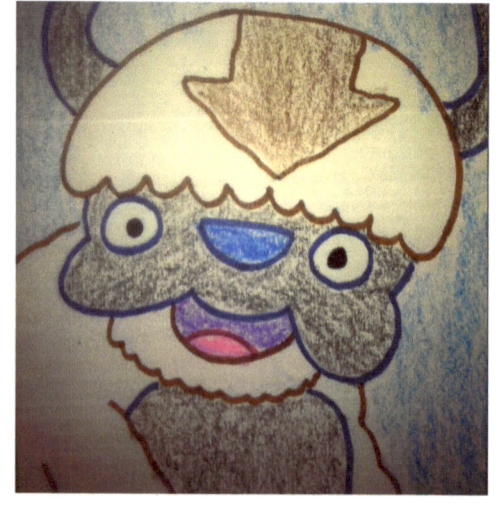

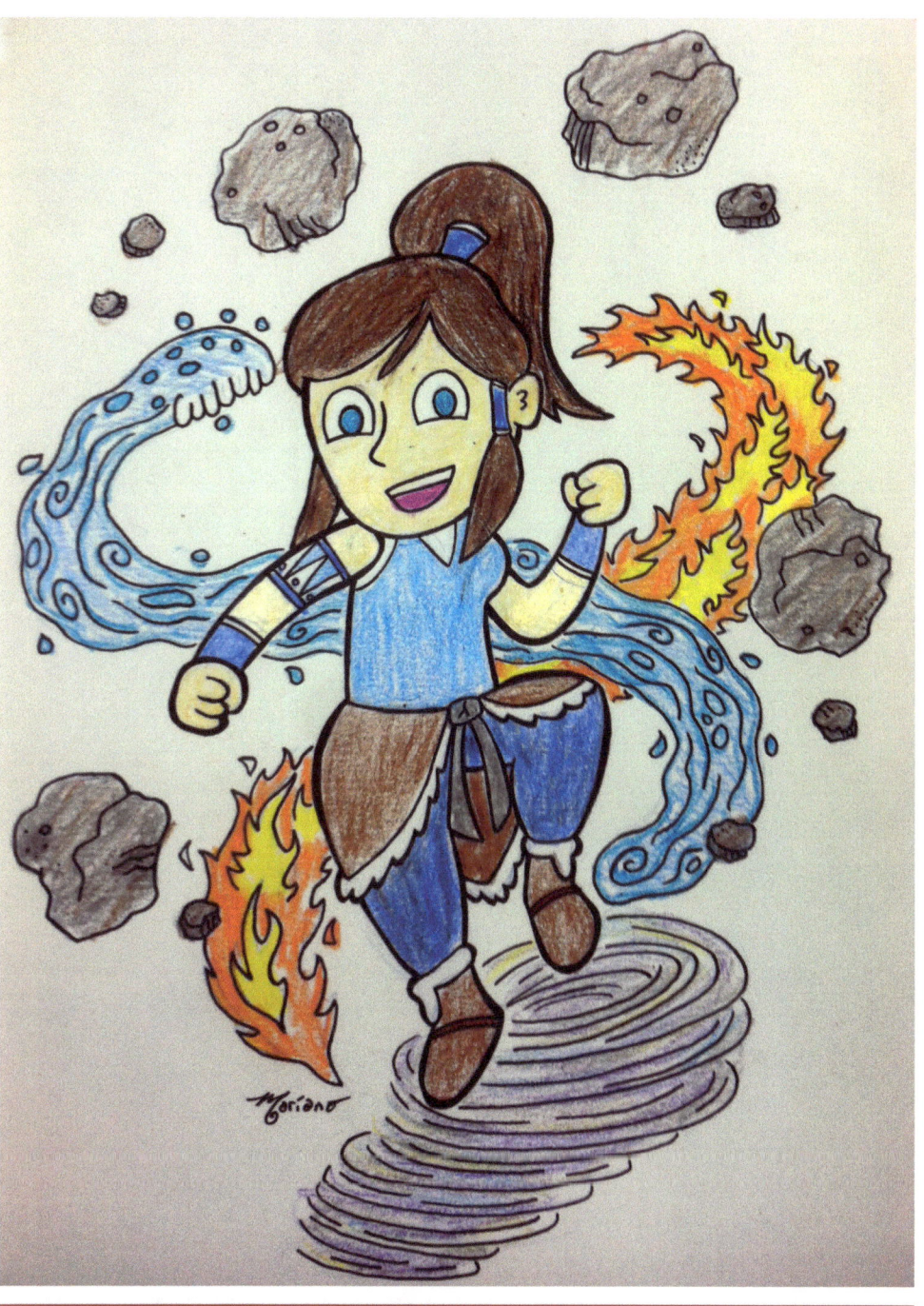

OTHER PAGE: Avatar Aang, Katara, Toph, Uncle Iroh, Appa

THIS PAGE: Avatar Korra

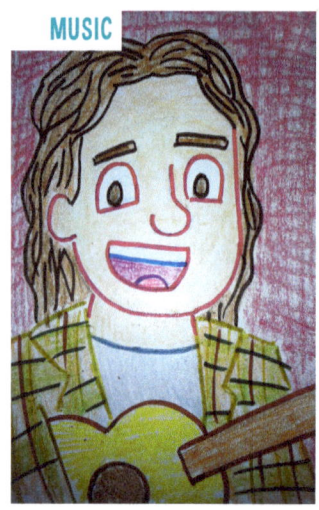

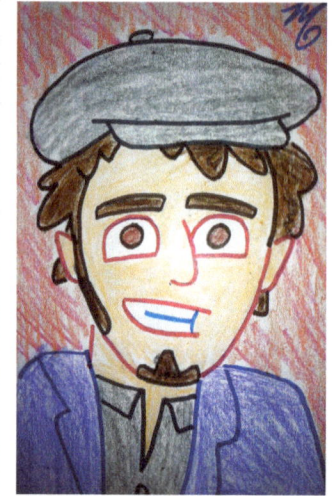

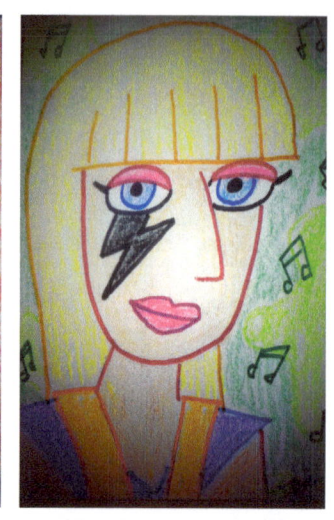

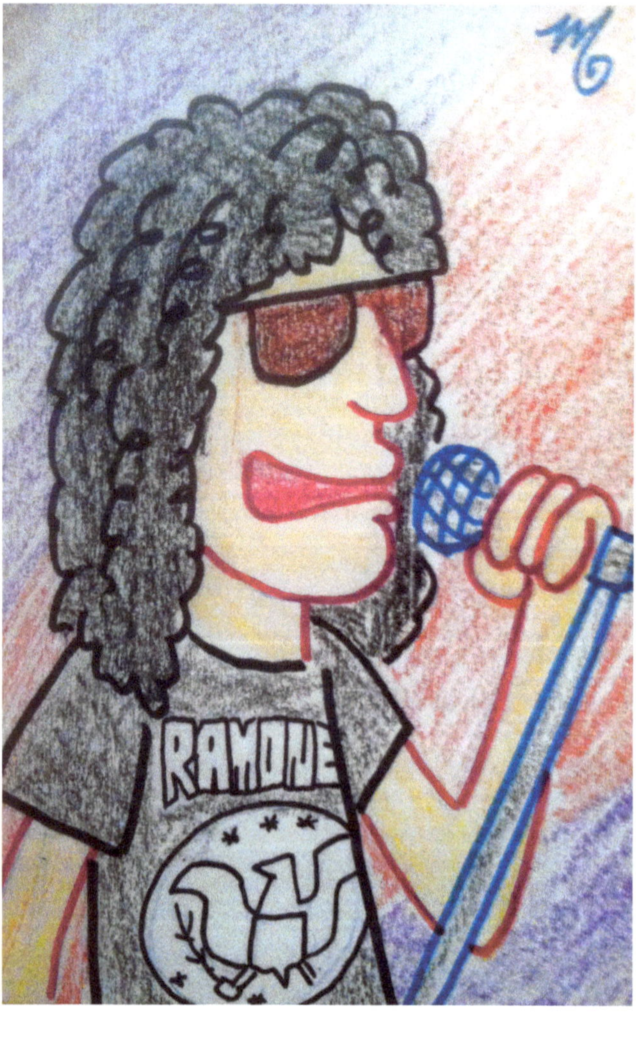

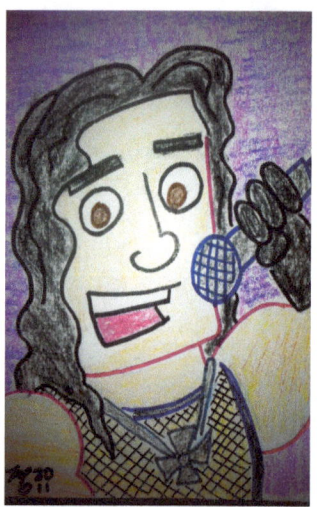

THIS PAGE:
Eddie Vedder
Tom Waits
Lady Gaga
Glen Danzig
Joey Ramone

OTHER PAGE:
Walter White
Jesse Pinkman
Frank Reynolds
Charlie Kelly

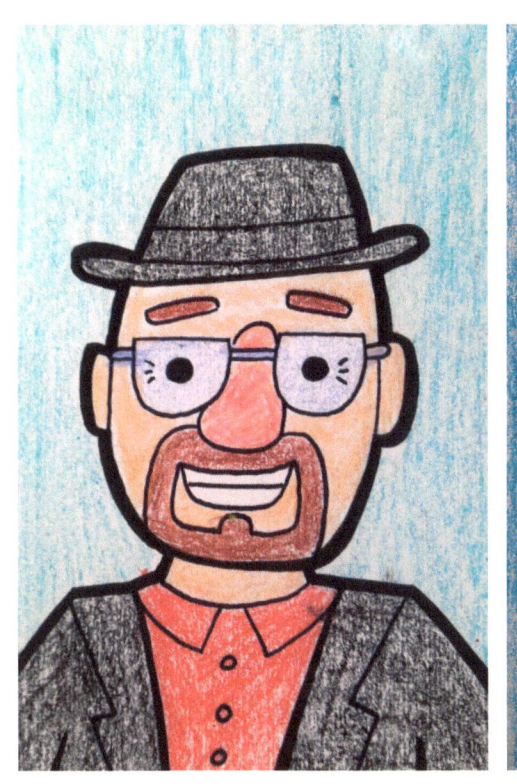
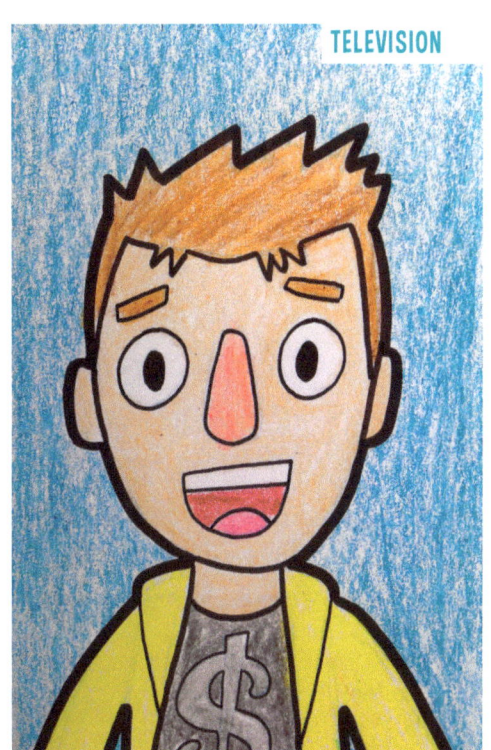
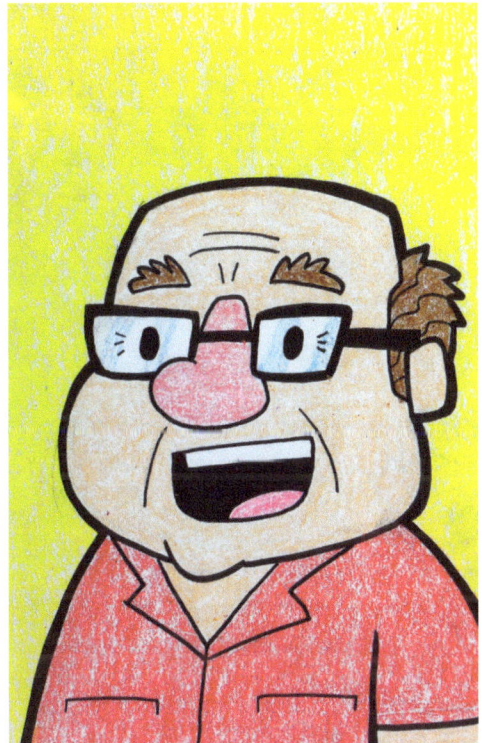
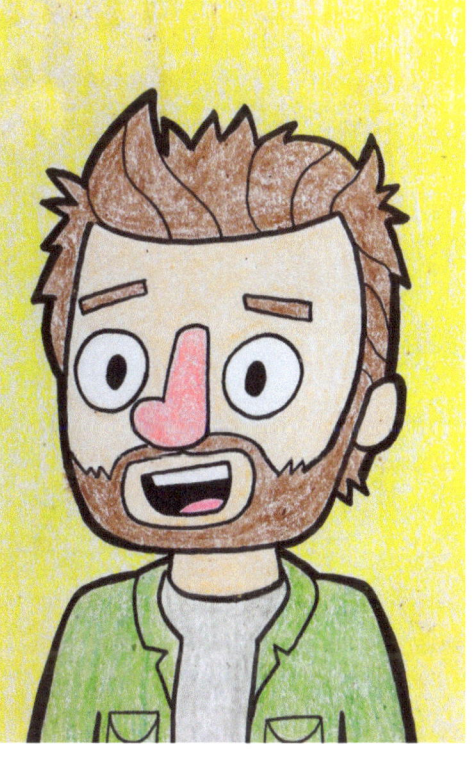

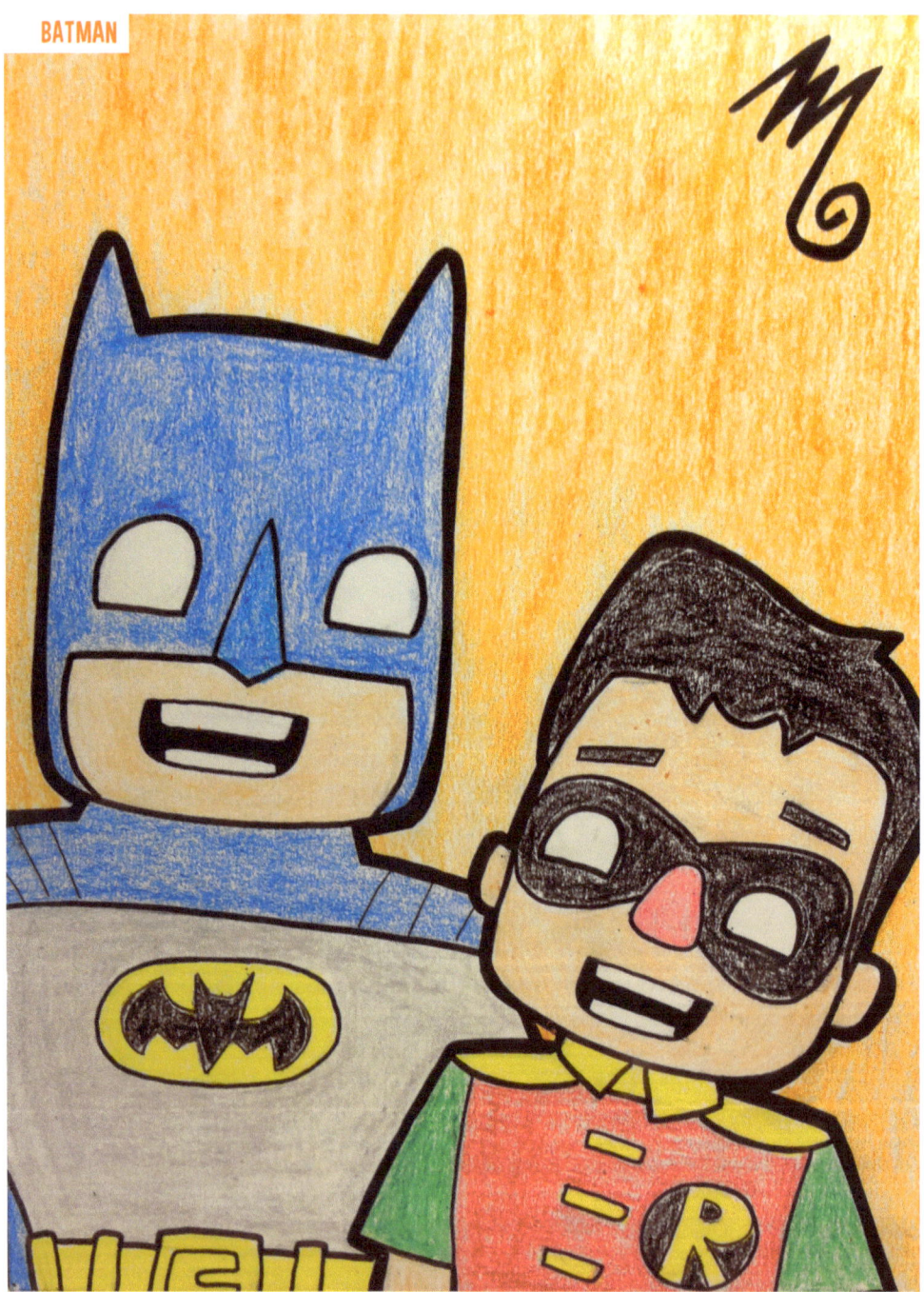

THIS PAGE: Batman and Robin

OTHER PAGE: Catwoman, Harley Quinn, Penguin vs Bat Penguin

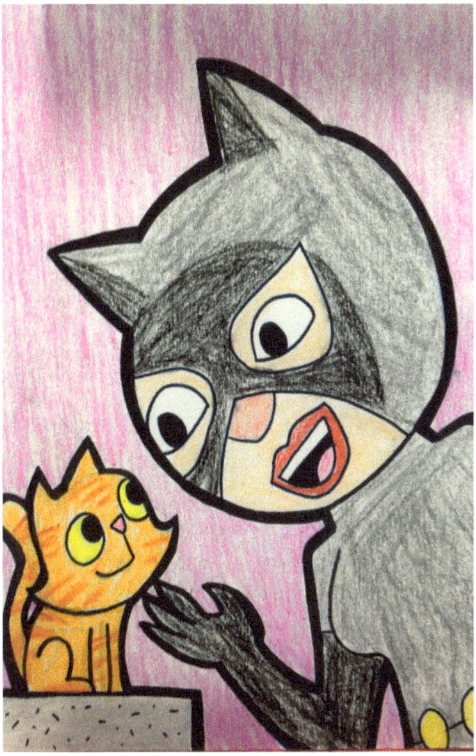
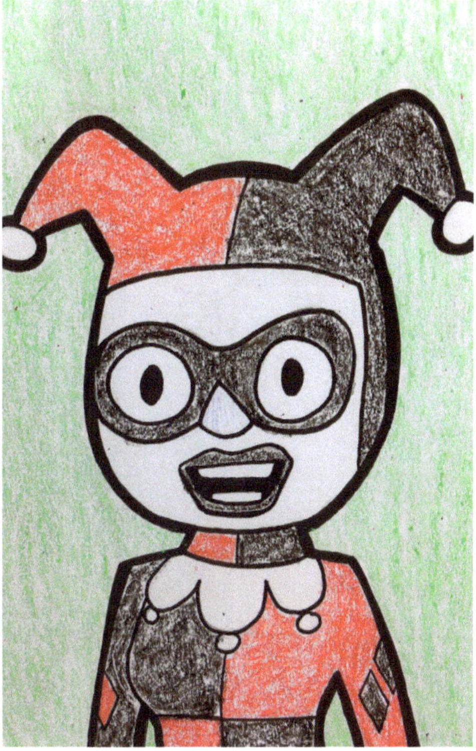
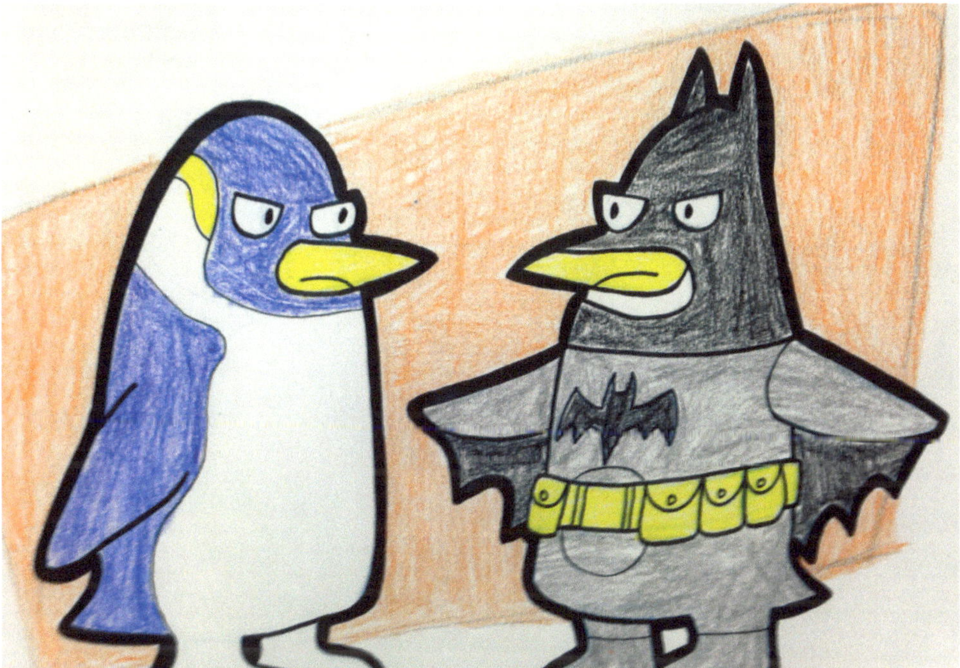

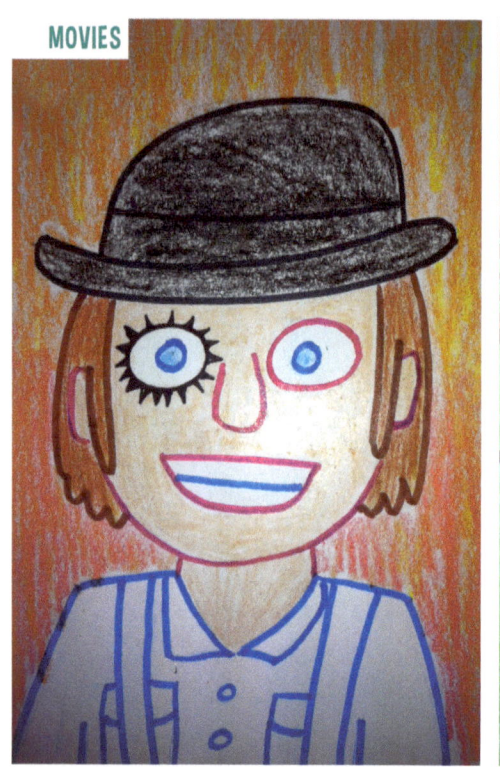

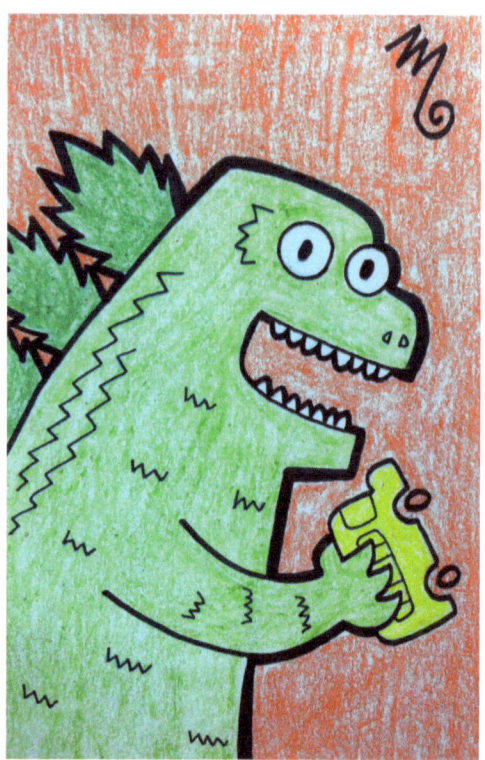

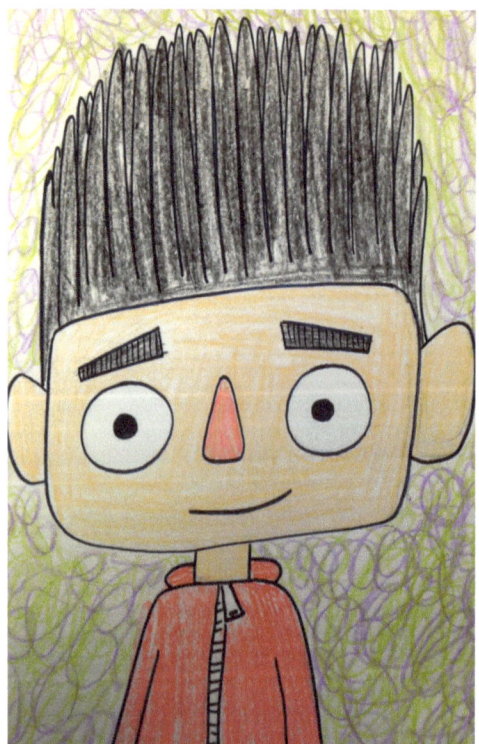

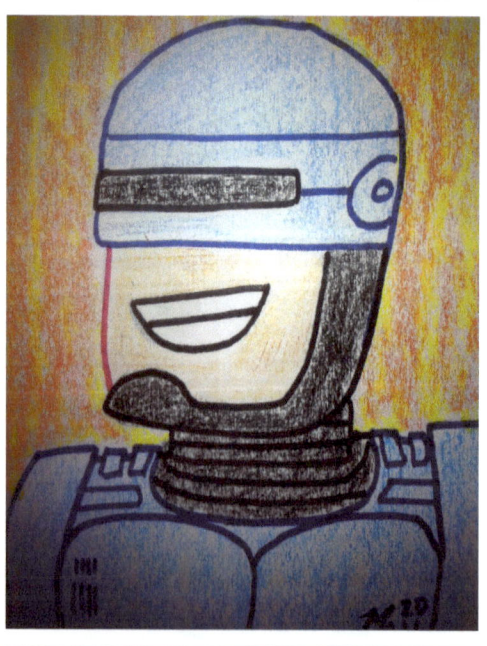

THIS PAGE: Alex, Godzilla, ParaNorman, RoboCop
OTHER PAGE: Cornelius, Black Dynamite,
Dorothy, Kano

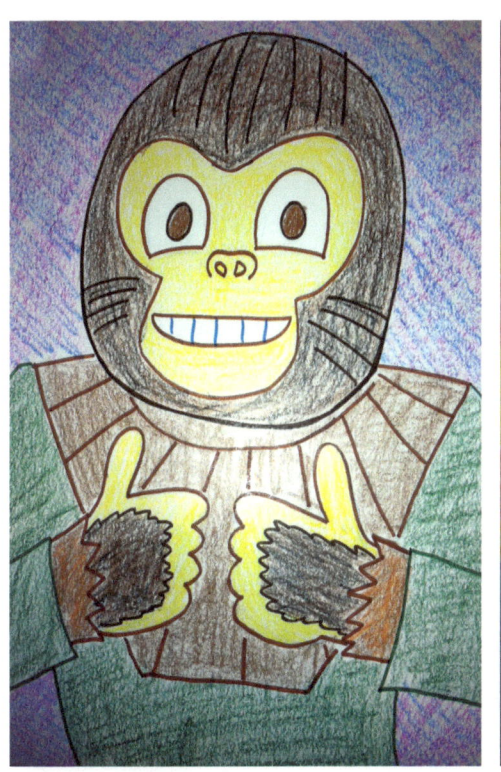

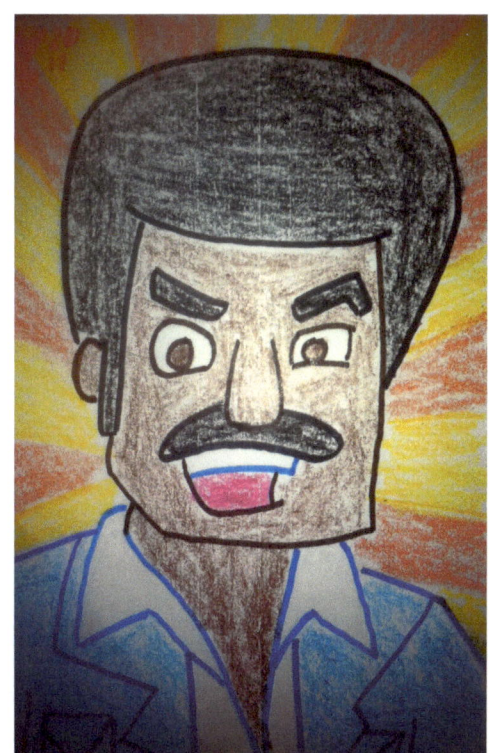

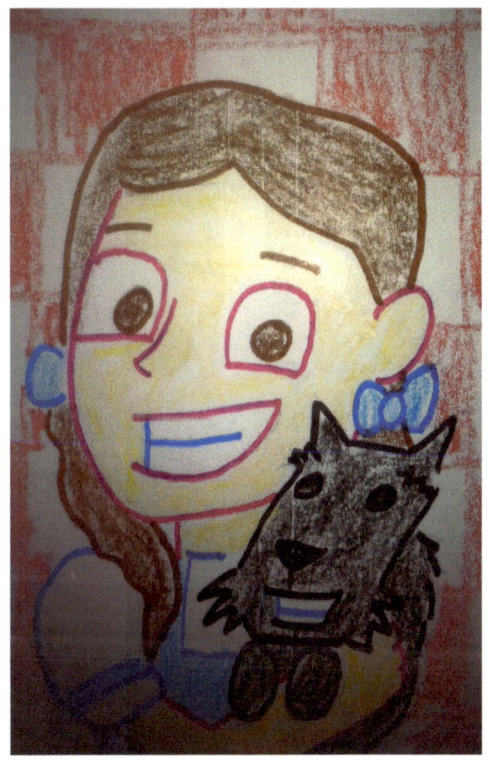

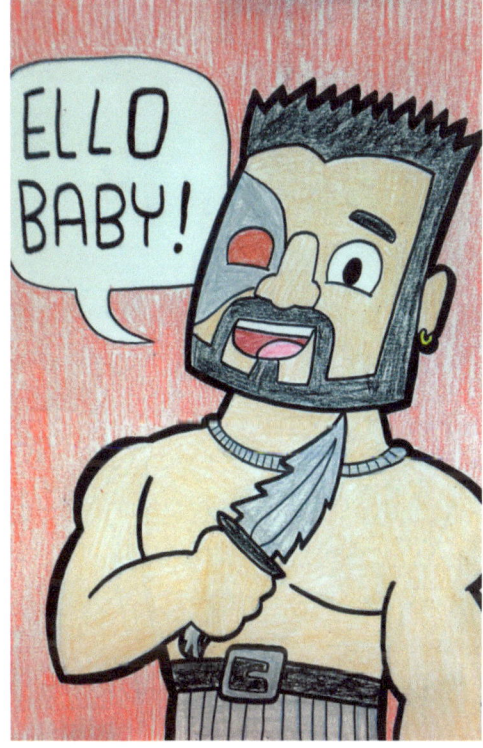

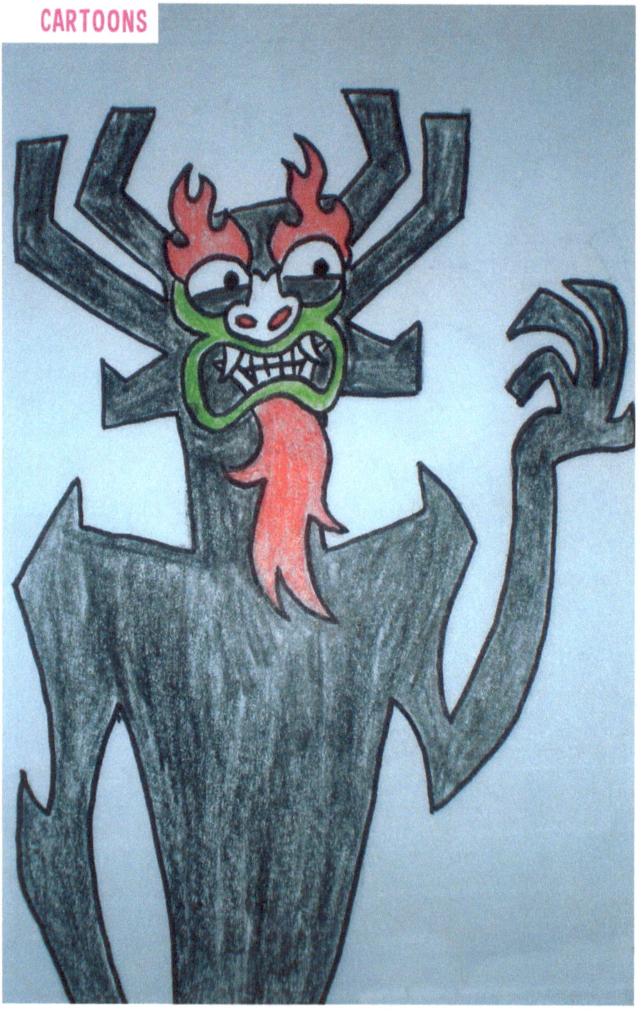

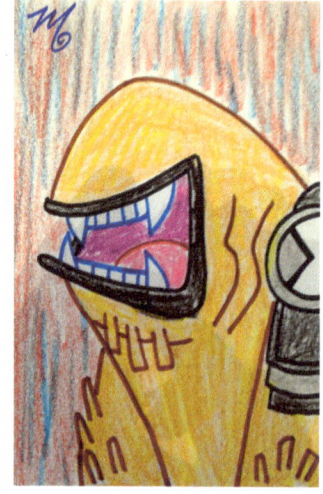

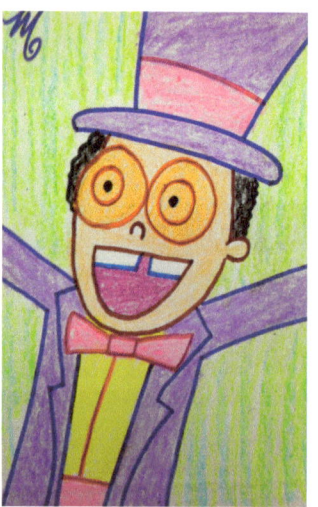

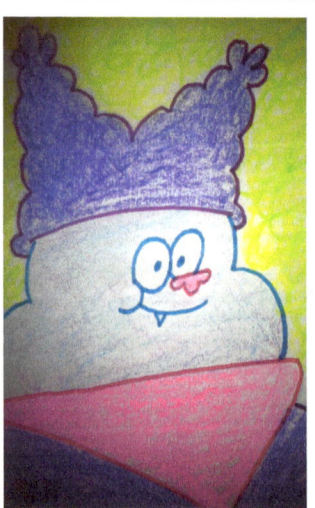

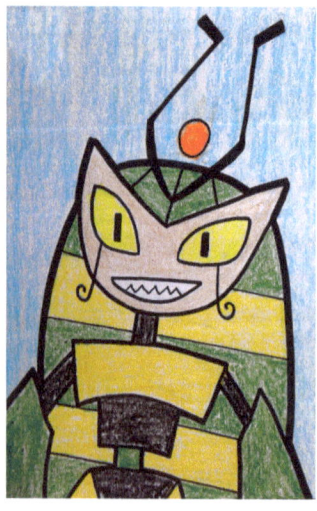

THIS PAGE:
Aku
Wildmutt
The Warden
Chowder
Vexus

OTHER PAGE:
Chuckles
Destro
Wilt
Ickis

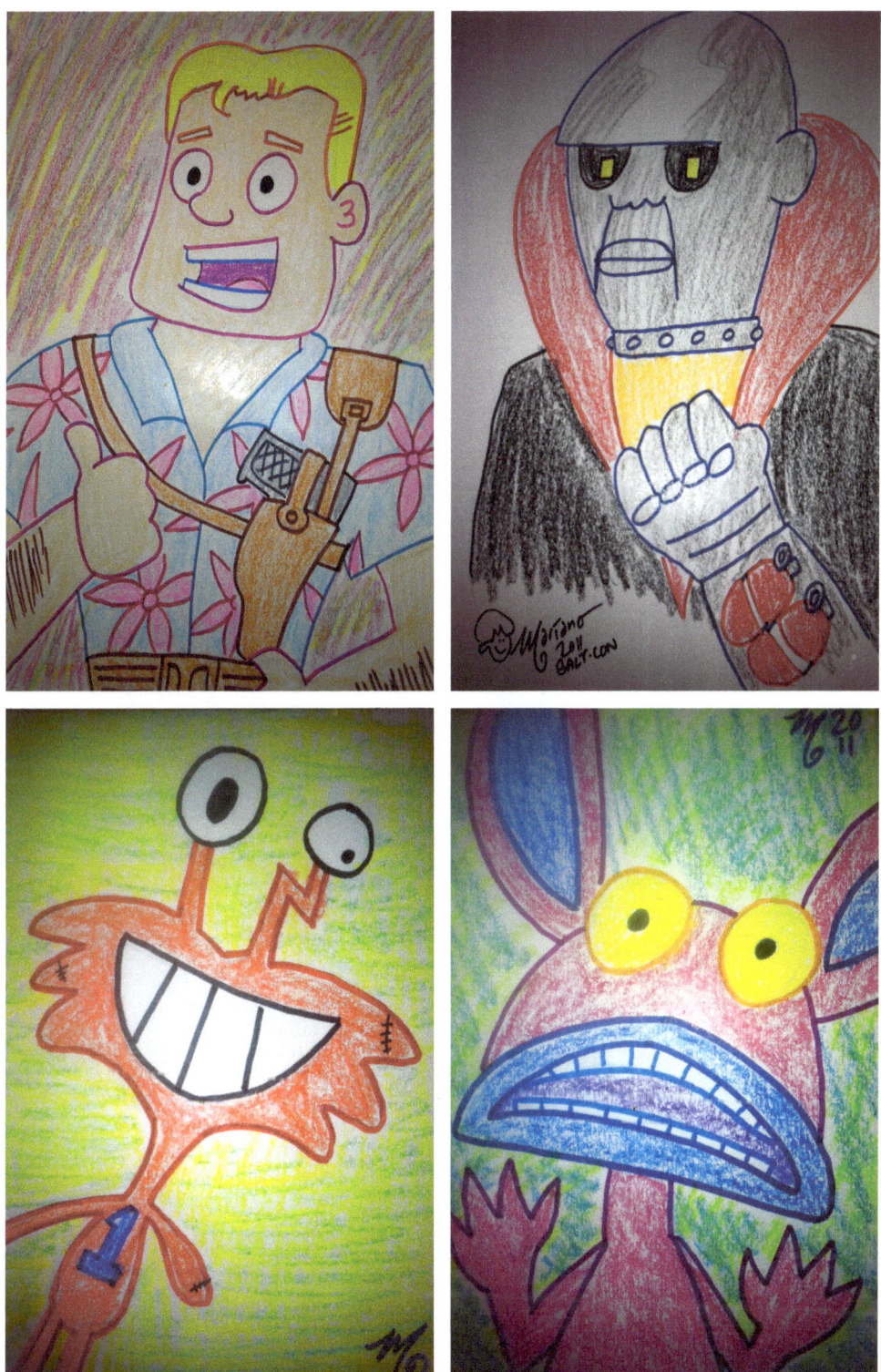

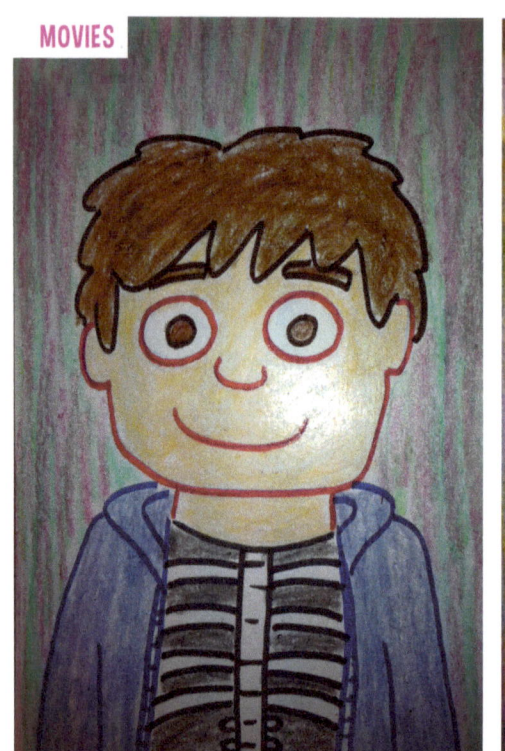
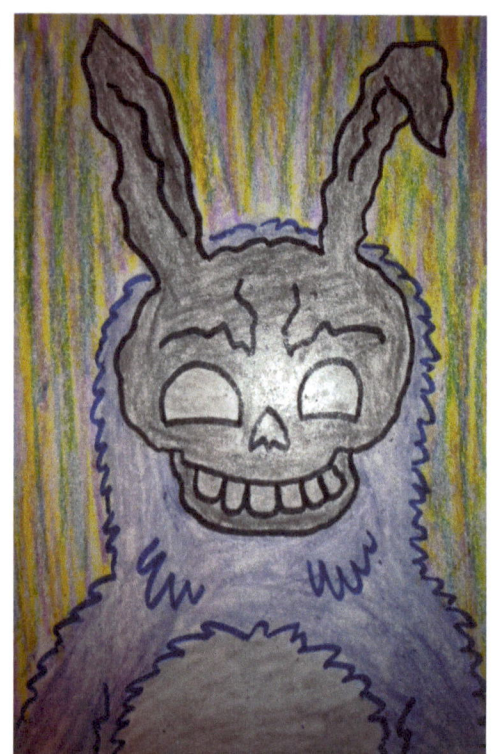
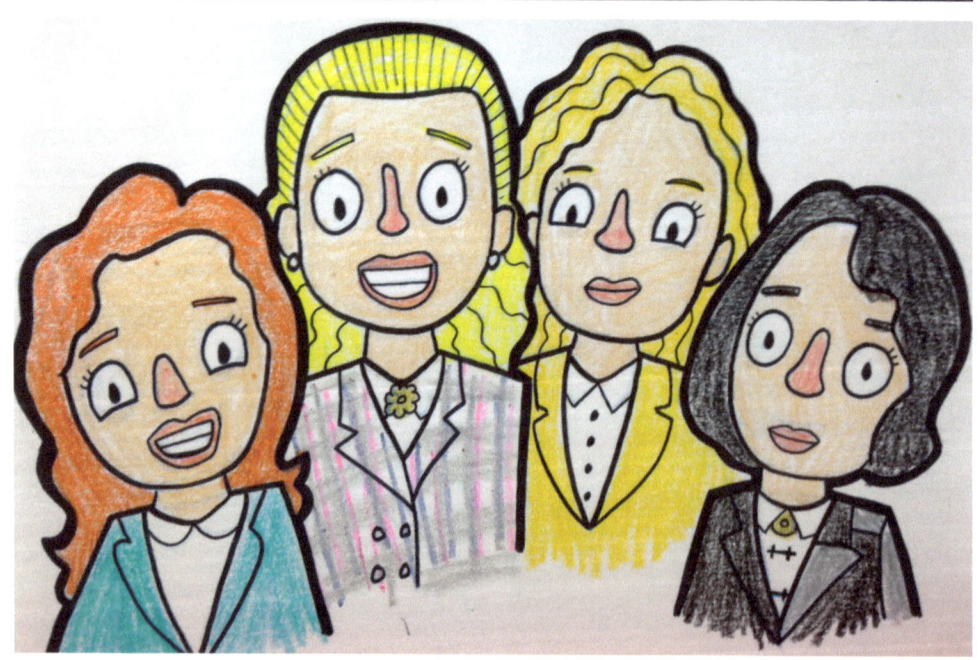

THIS PAGE: Donnie Darko, Frank the Bunny, Heathers
OTHER PAGE: Yoda Doing Yoga

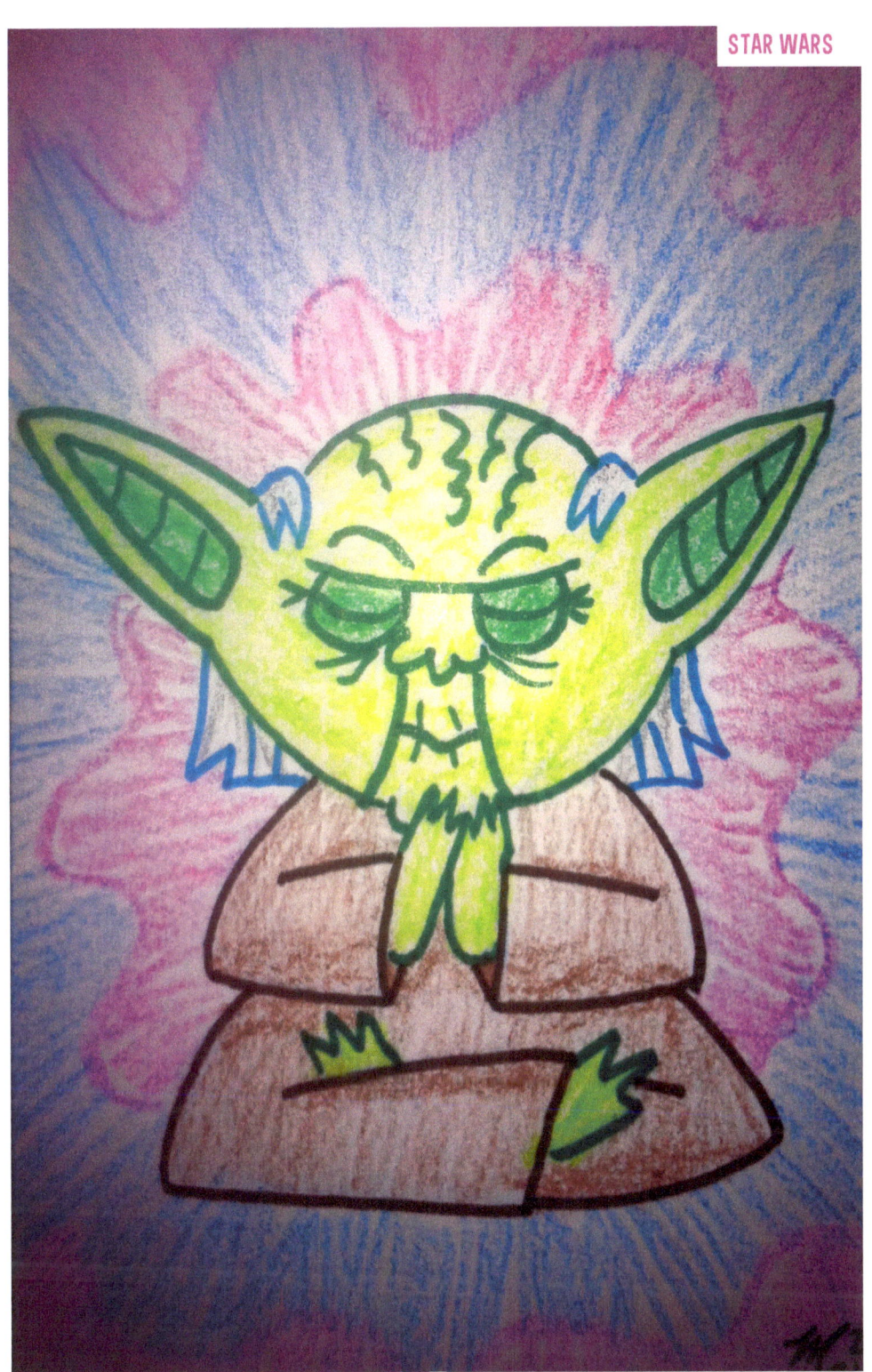

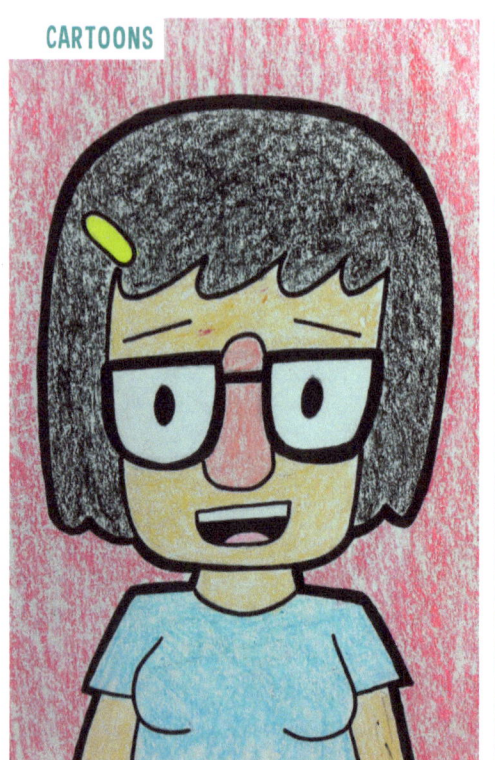
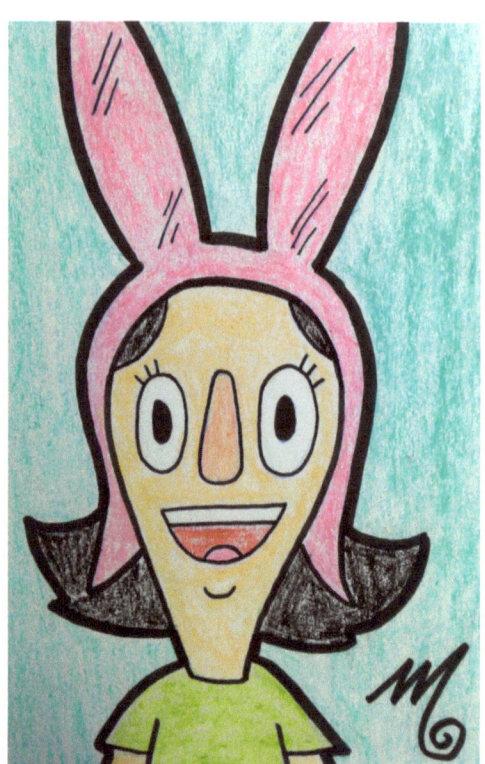

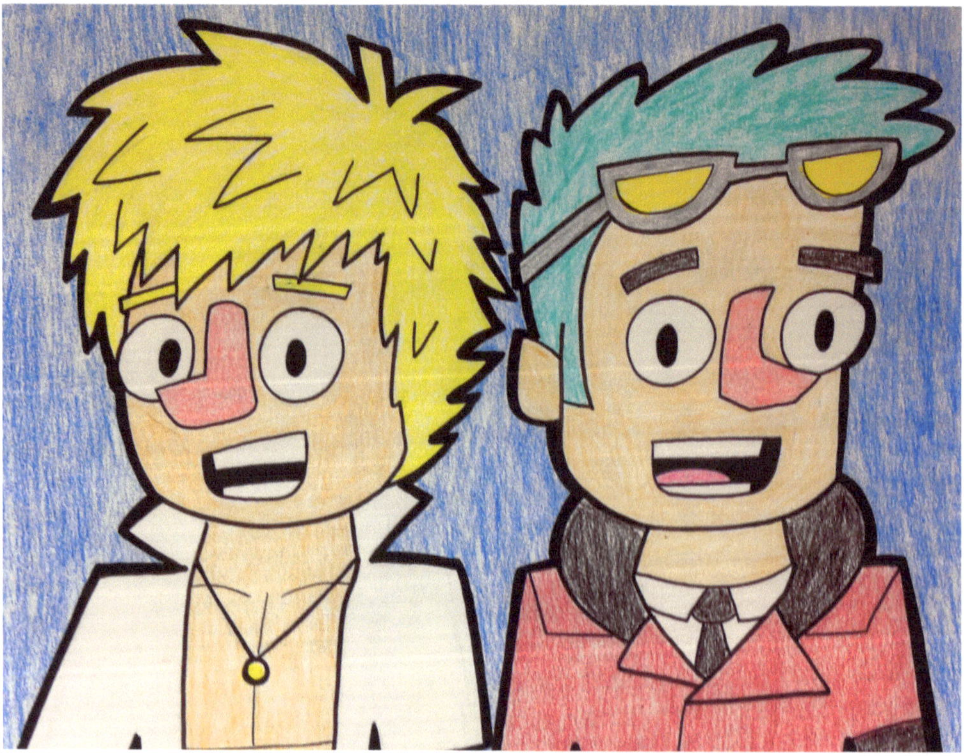

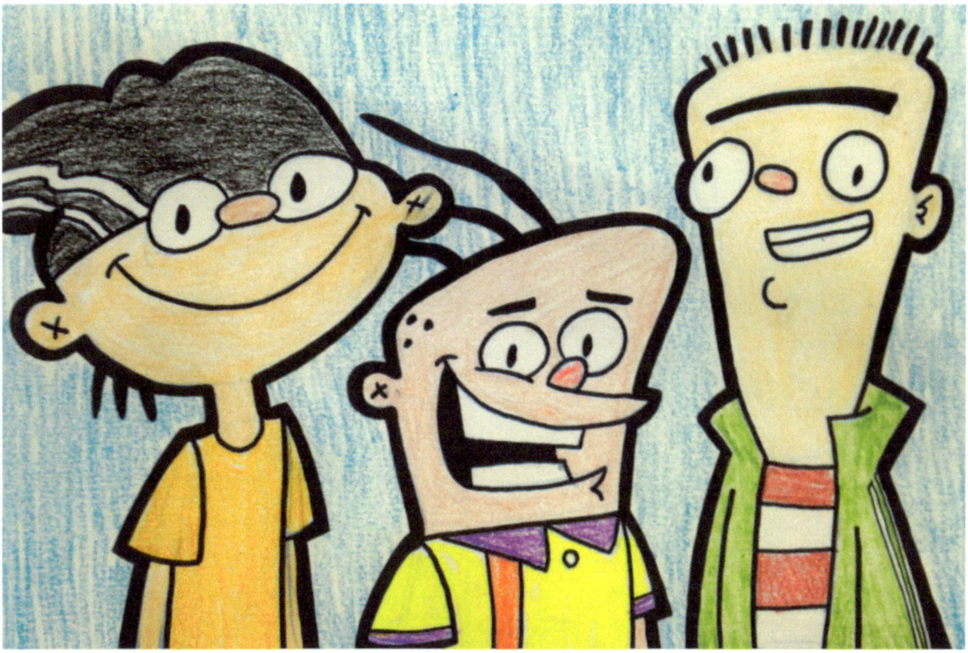

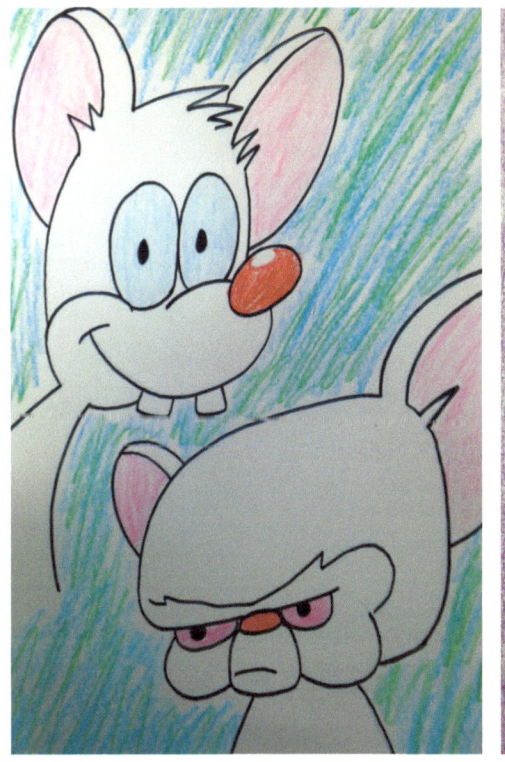

OTHER PAGE: Tina Belcher, Louise Belcher, Sun and Neptune
THIS PAGE: Ed, Edd, and Eddy, Pinky and The Brain, Dan

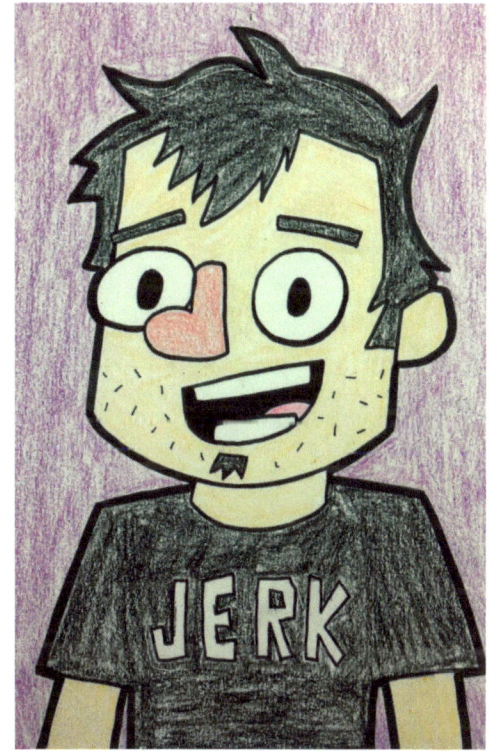

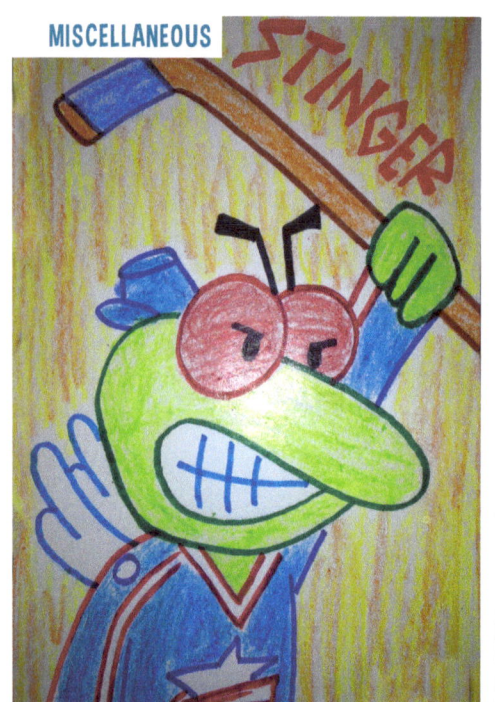

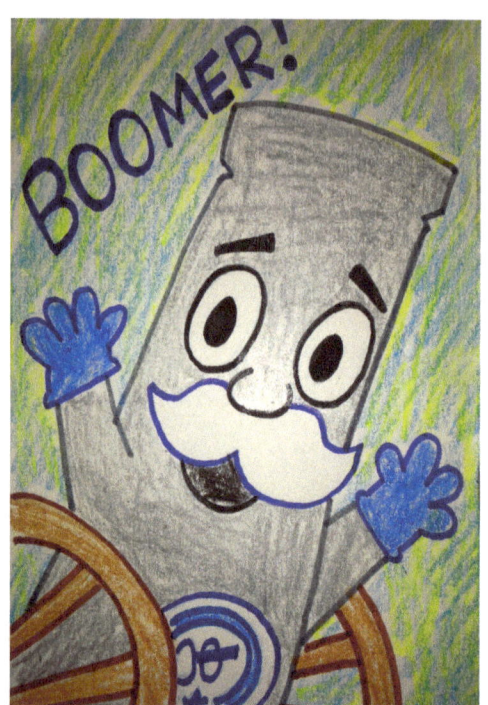

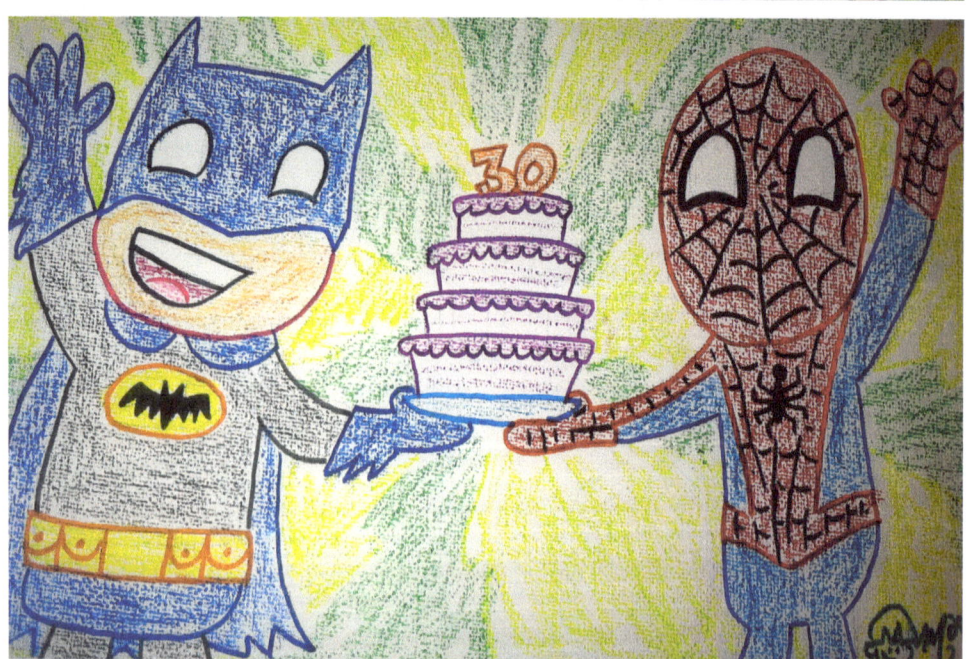

THIS PAGE: Stinger, Boomer, Batman and Spider-Man Birthday Greeting

OTHER PAGE: Narwhal, Charles Bukowski, Blue Lantern Spider-Man, Green Lantern Disco Stu

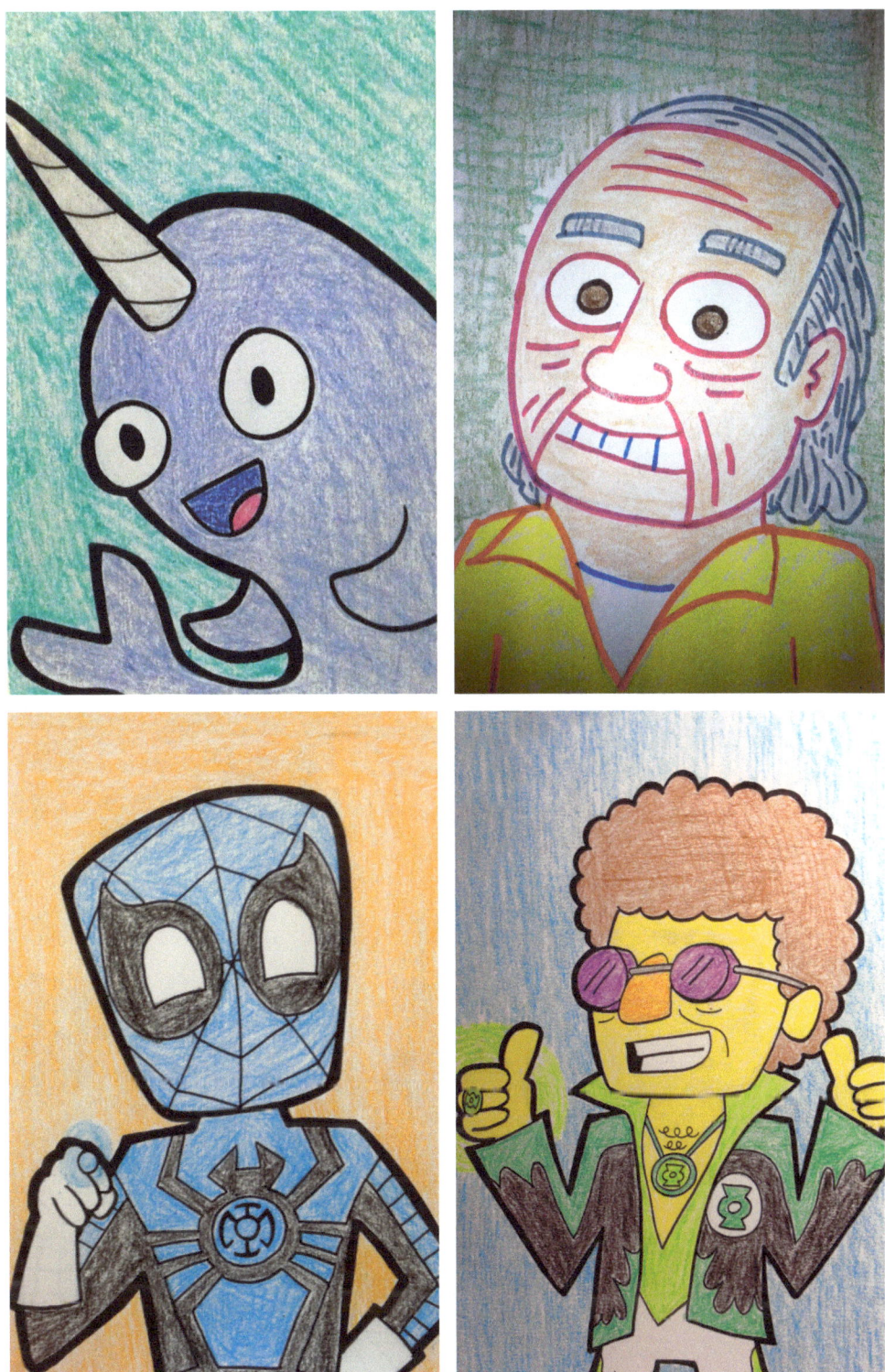

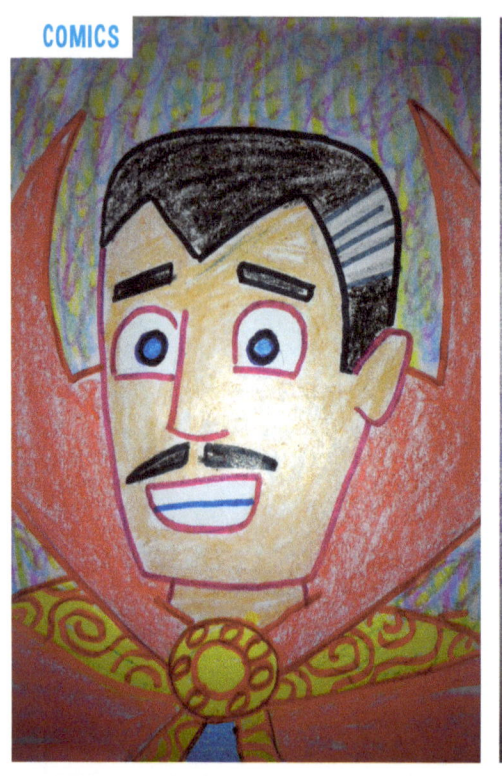
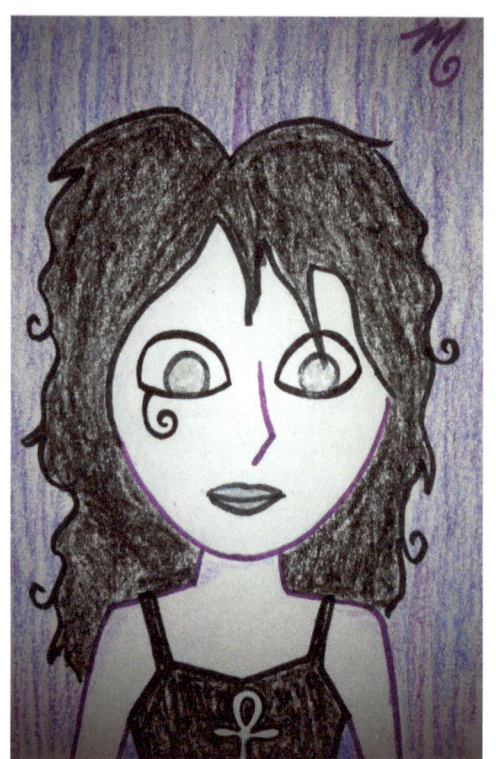
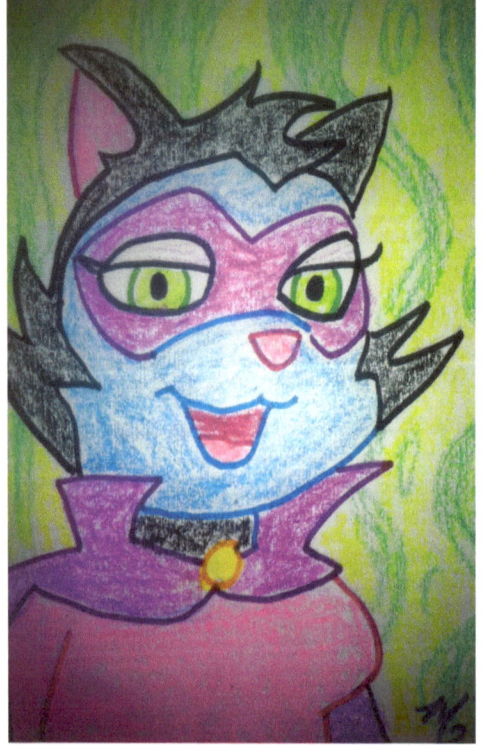
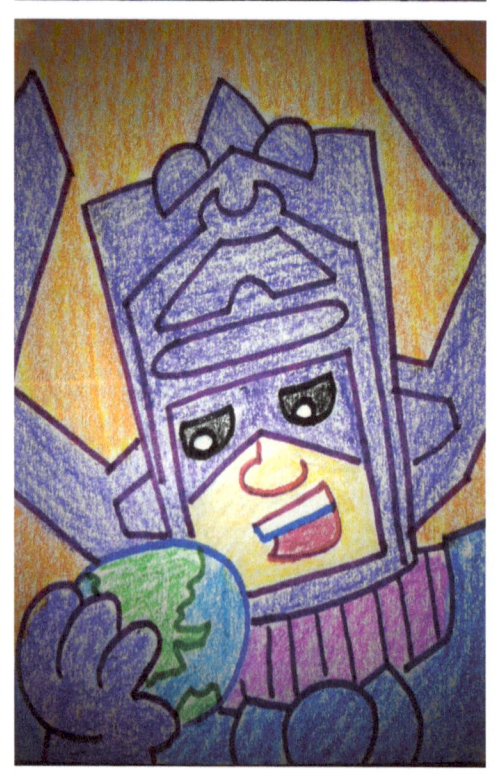

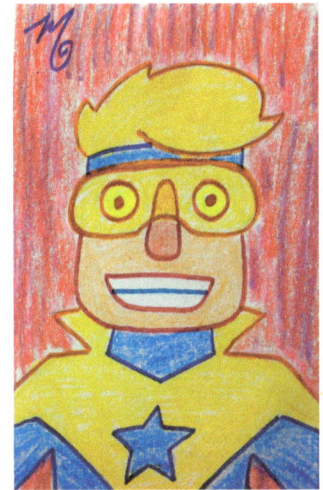

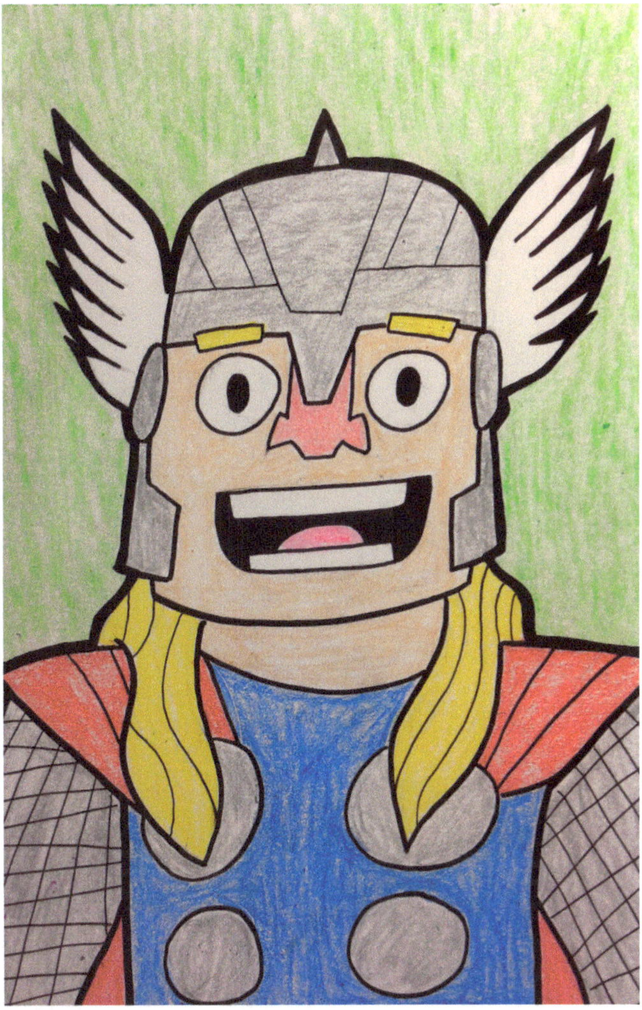

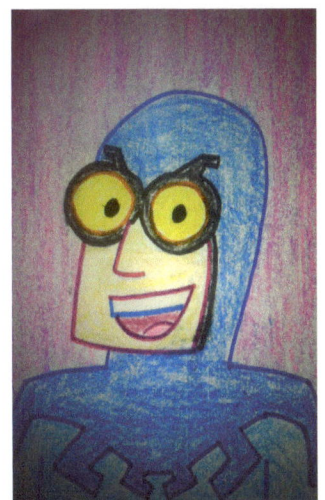

OTHER PAGE:
Dr. Strange
Death
Alley-Kat-Abra
Galactus

THIS PAGE:
Booster Gold
Blue Beetle
Thor
Ms. Marvel
Thanos

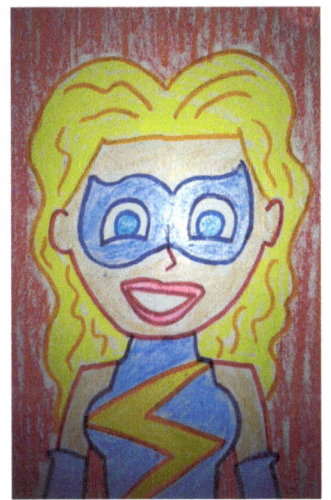

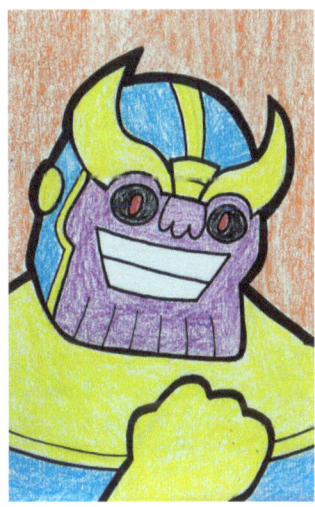

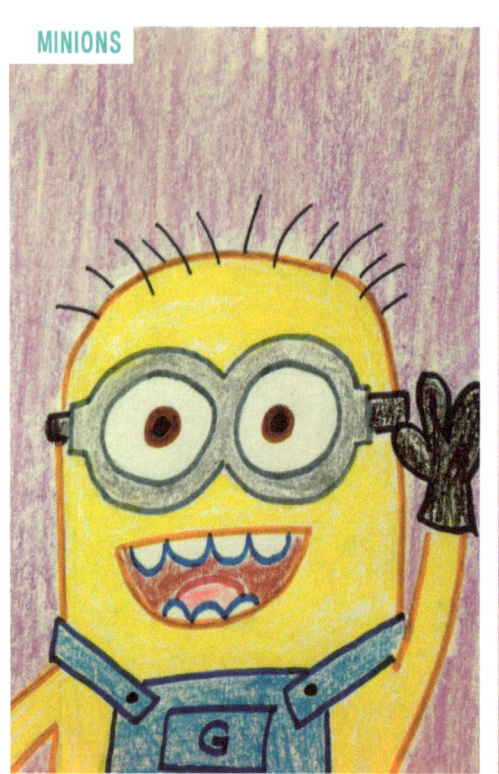
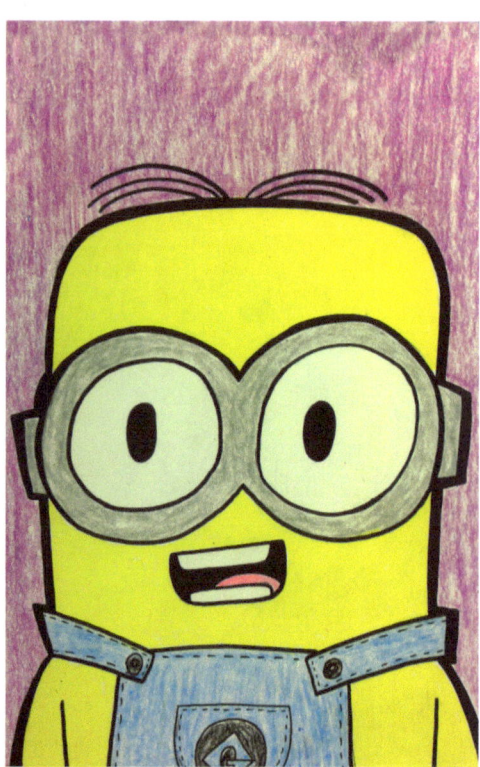
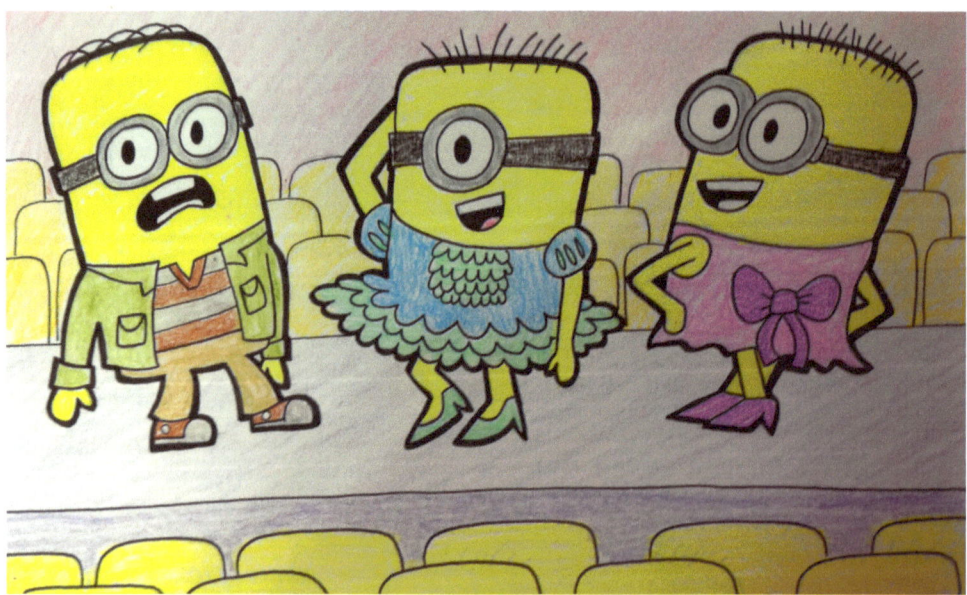

THIS PAGE: Phil, Dave, Minion Fashion Show

OTHER PAGE: Phineas, Perry, and Ferb, Agent P, Dr. Doofenshmirtz

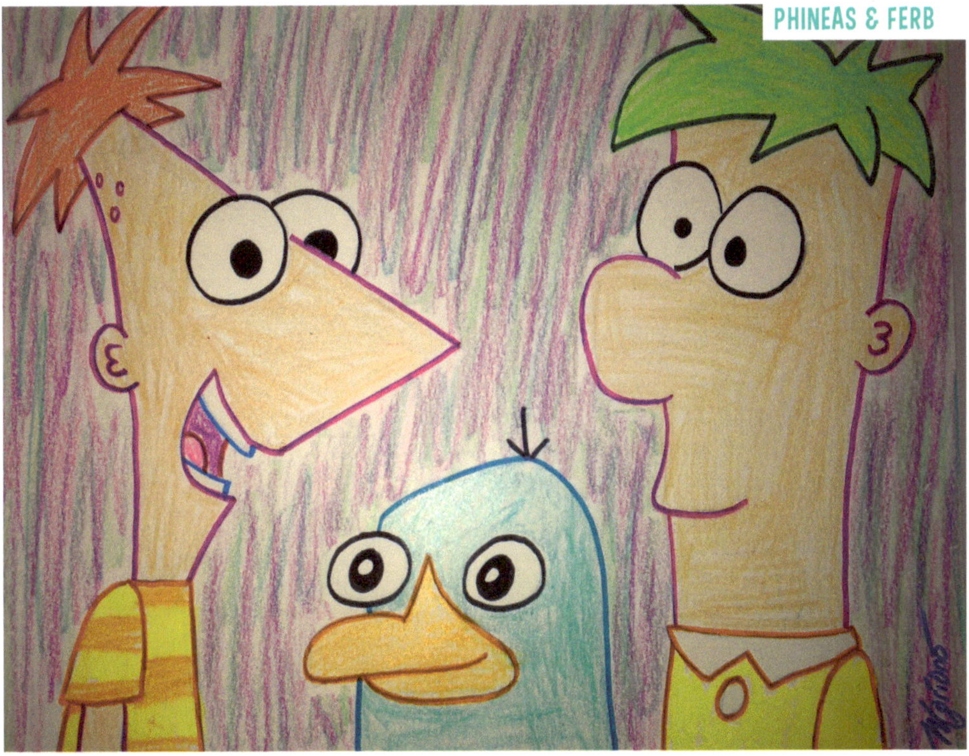

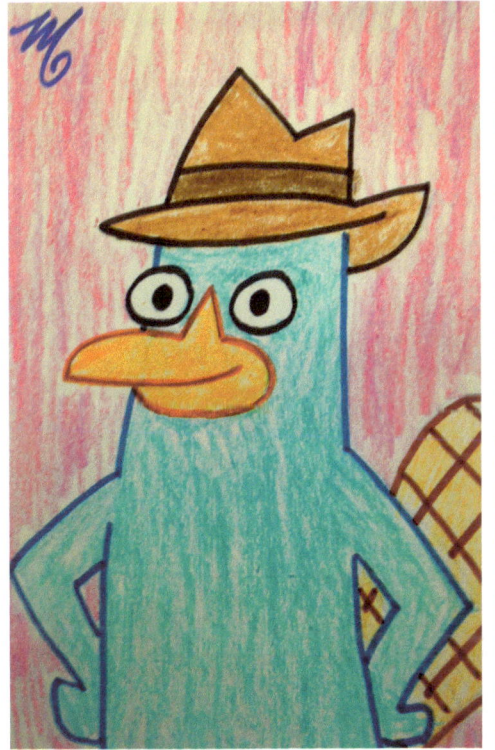

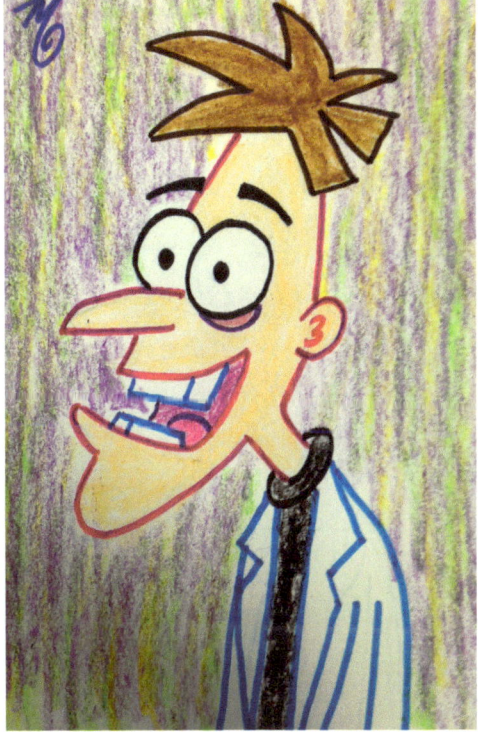

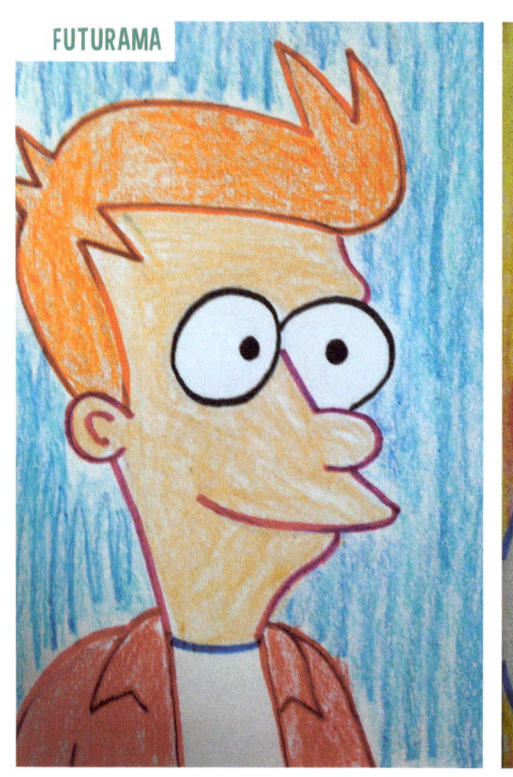
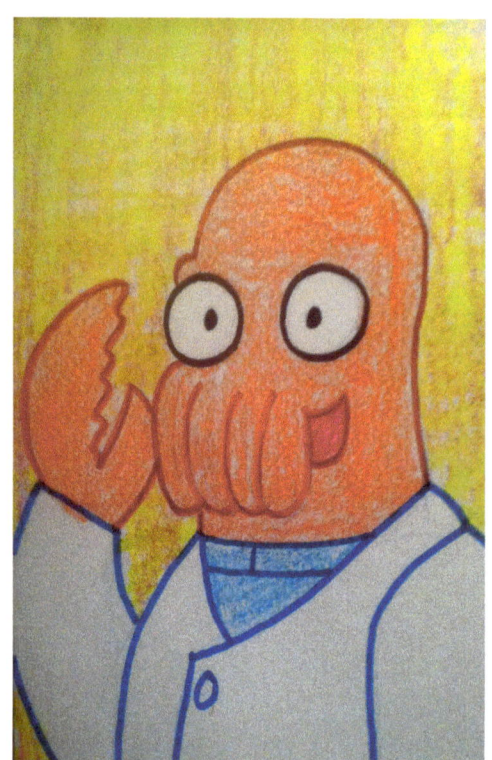
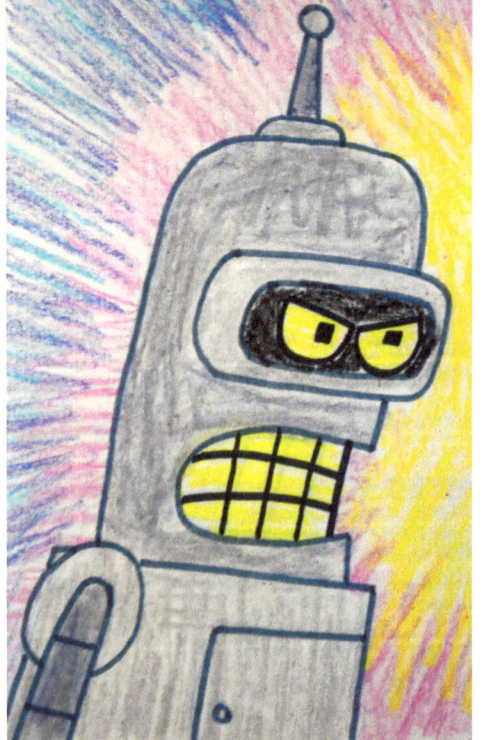
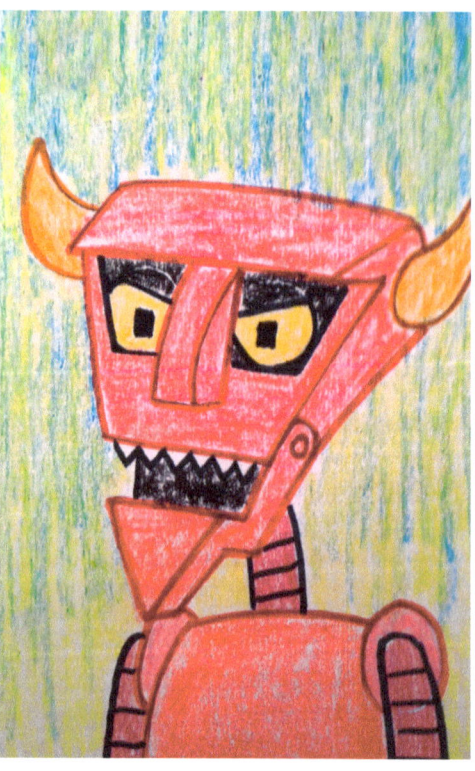

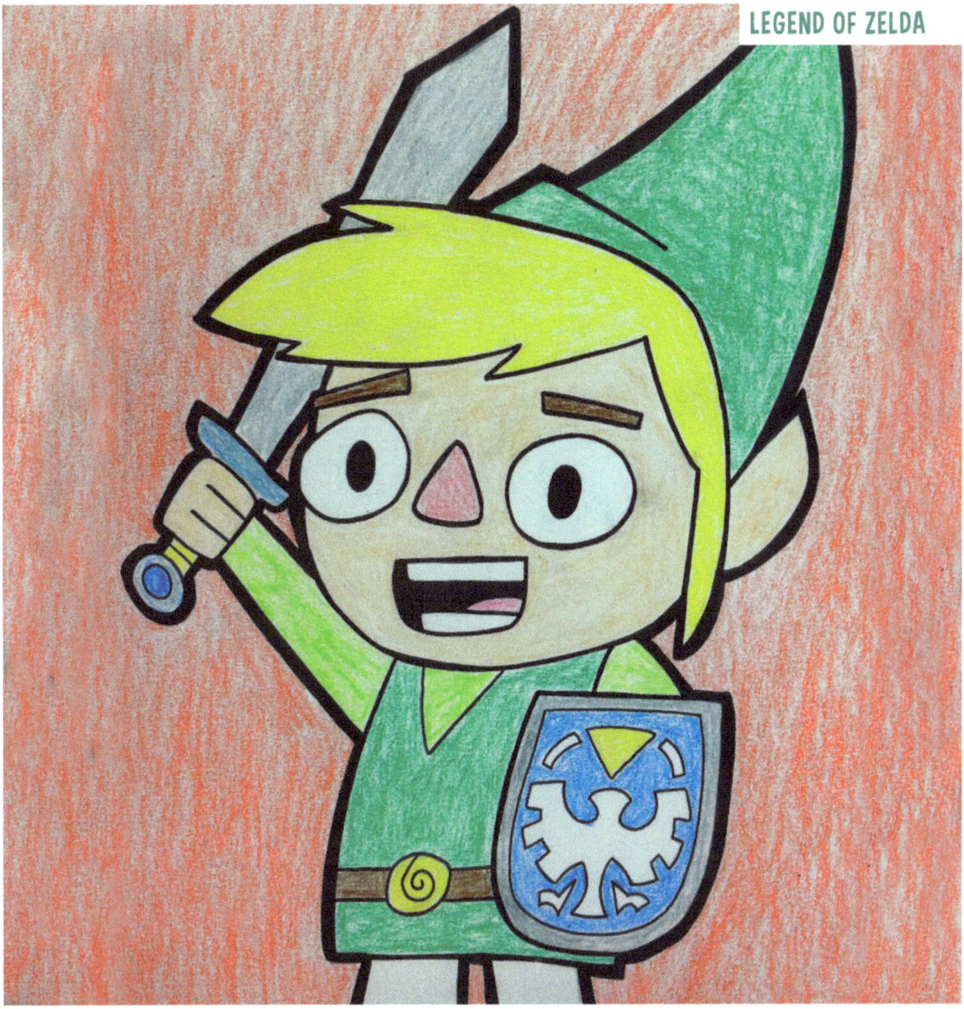

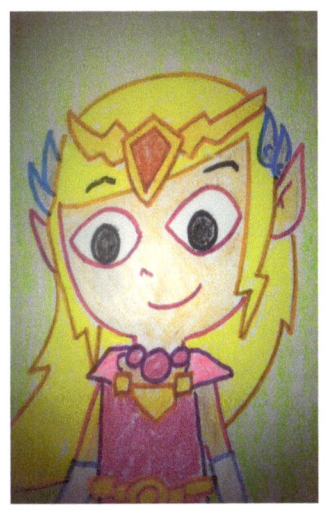

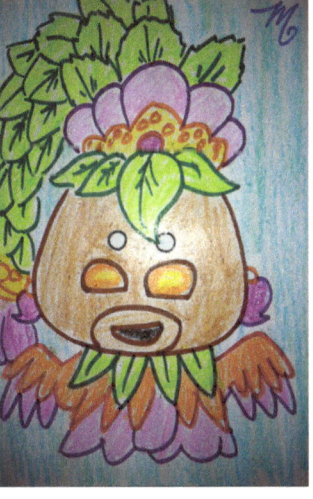

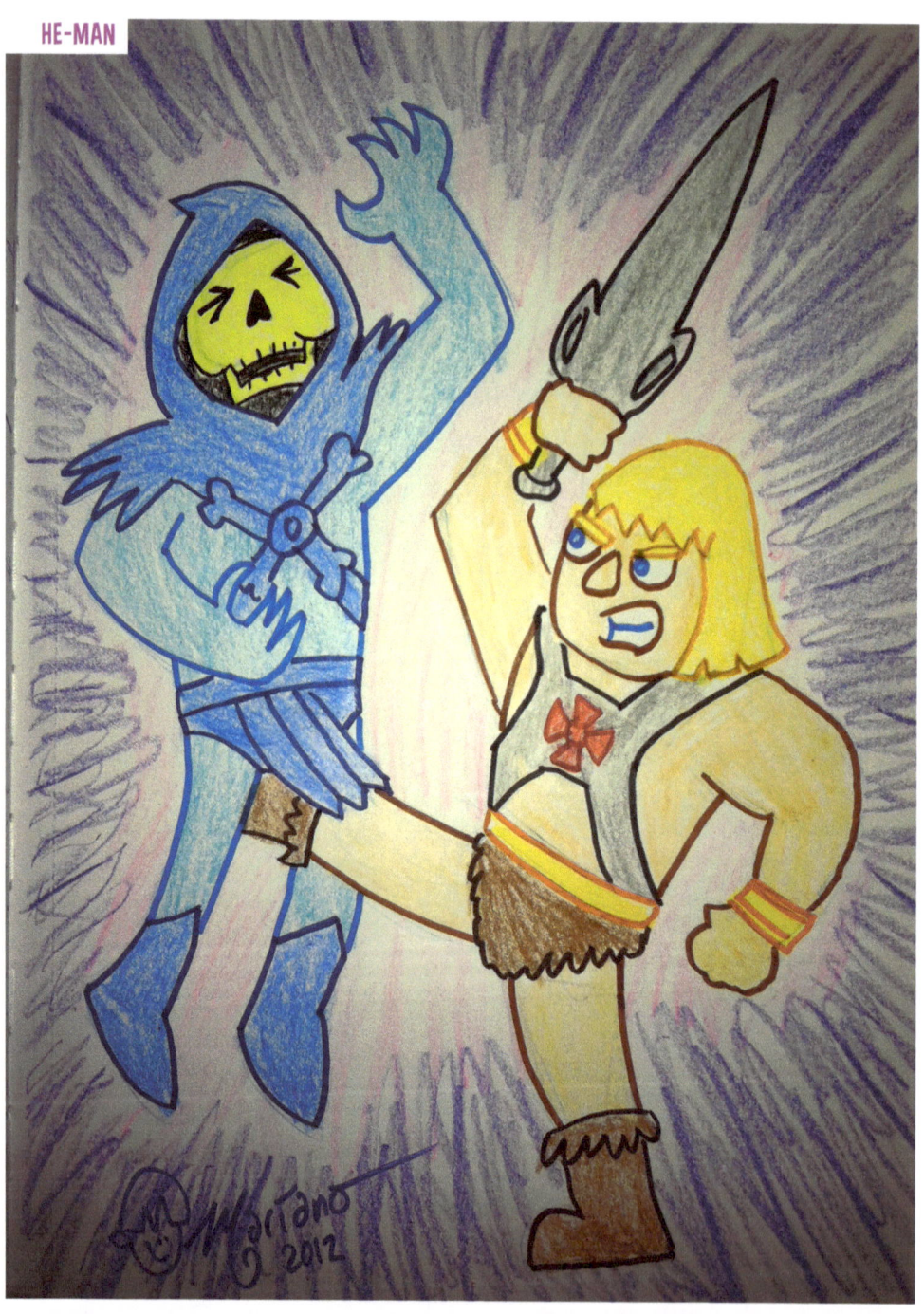

THIS PAGE: The Kick For Eternia

OTHER PAGE: Mer-Man, Skeletor, He-Man vs Lion-O

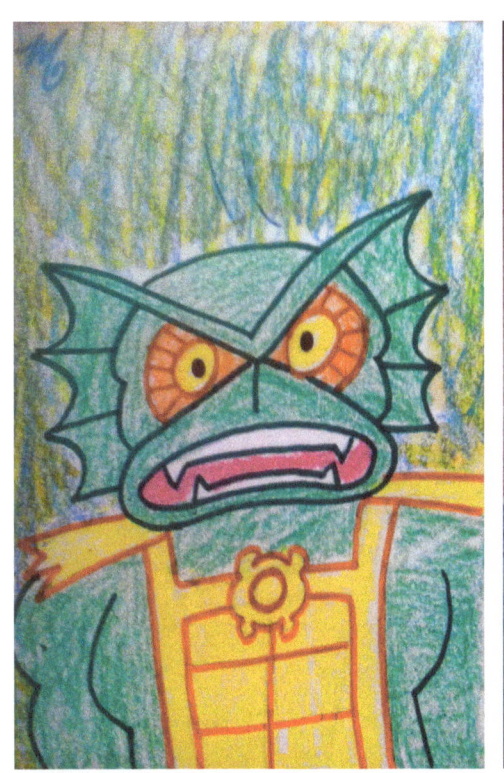
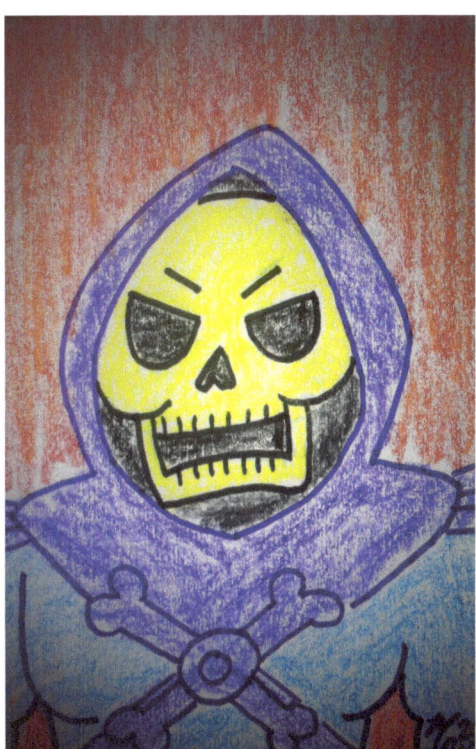

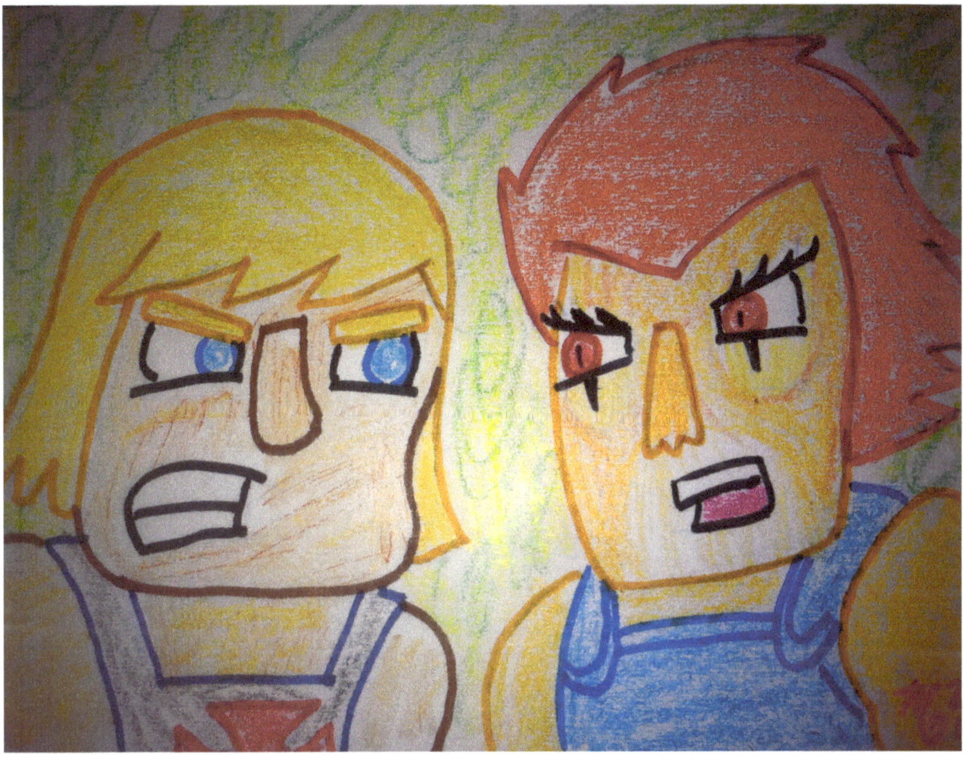

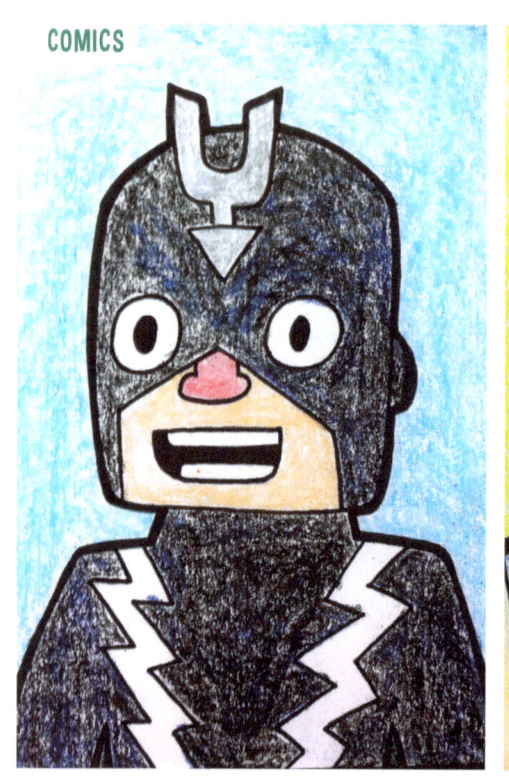

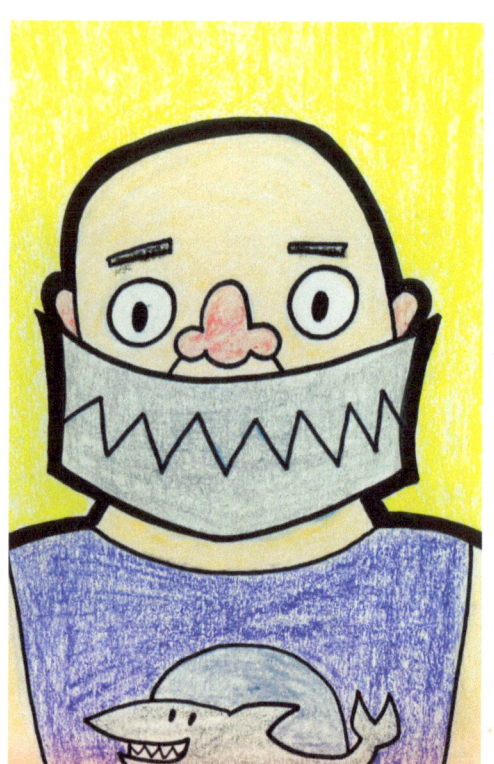

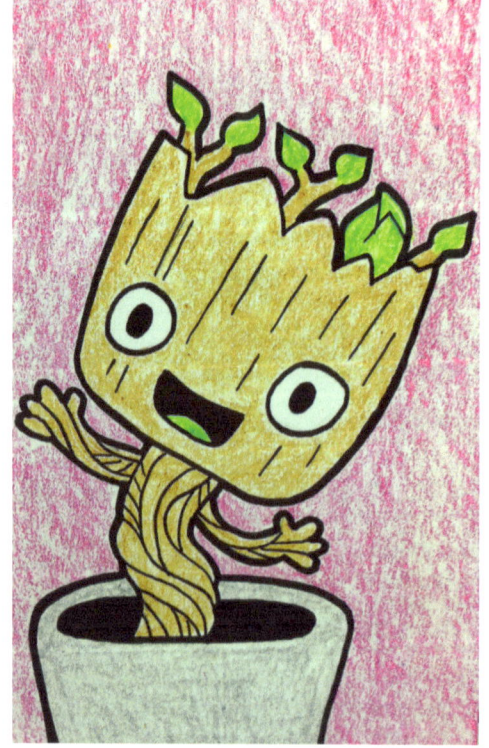

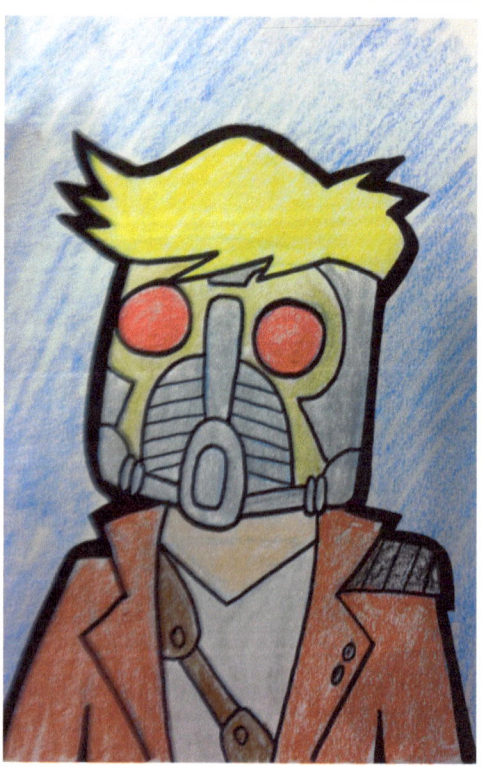

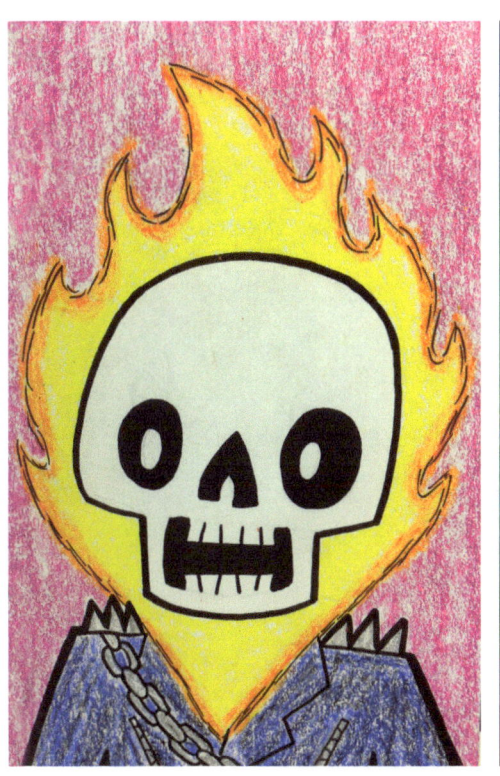
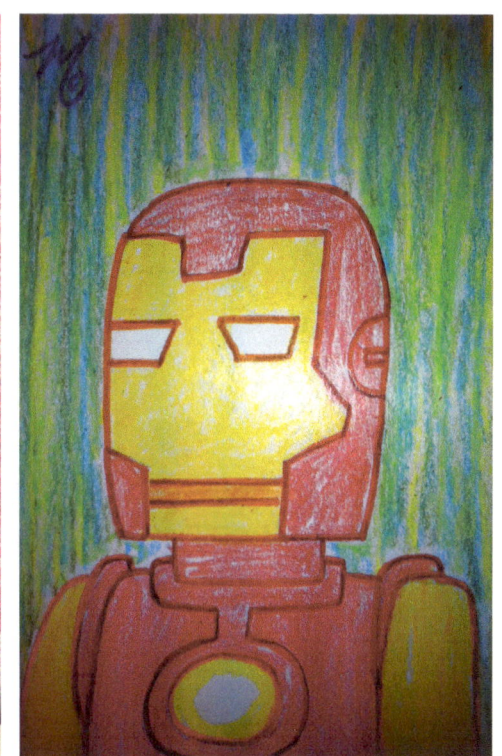
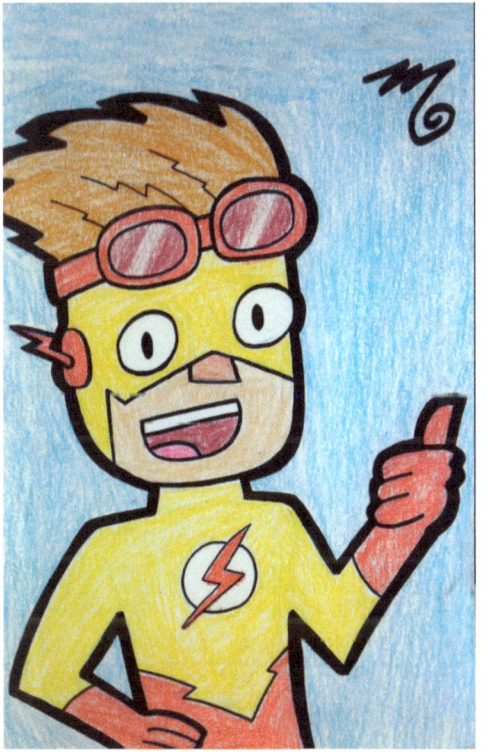
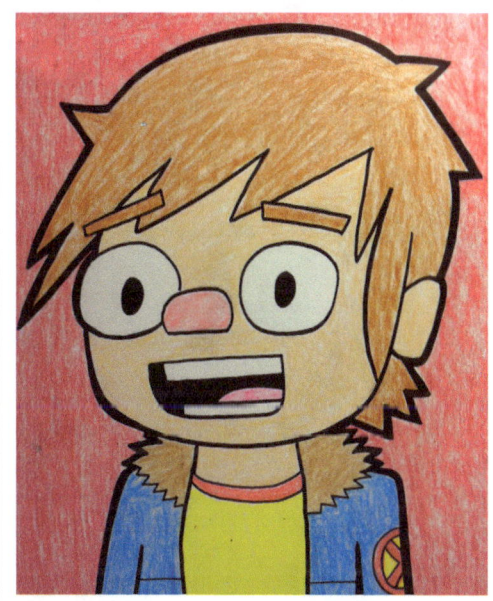

OTHER PAGE: Black Bolt, Jaws,
Baby Groot, Star Lord
THIS PAGE: Ghost Rider, Iron Man,
Kid Flash, Scott Pilgrim

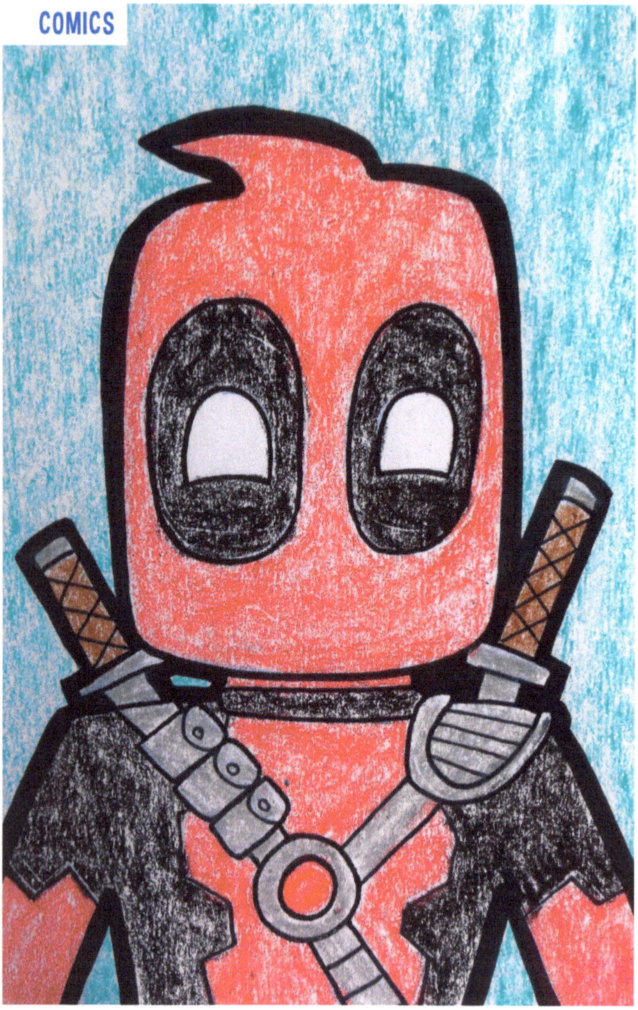

COMICS

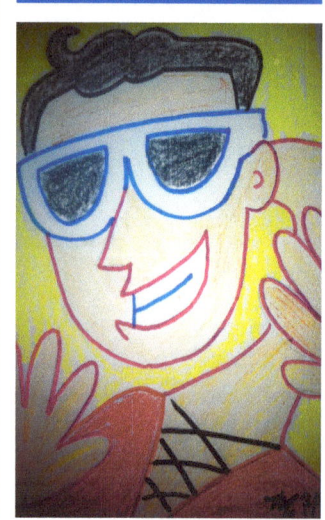

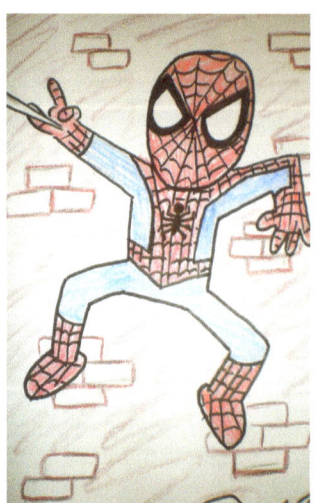

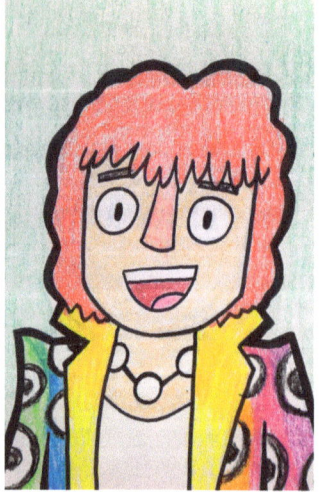

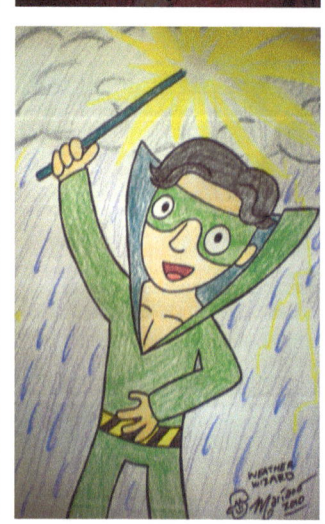

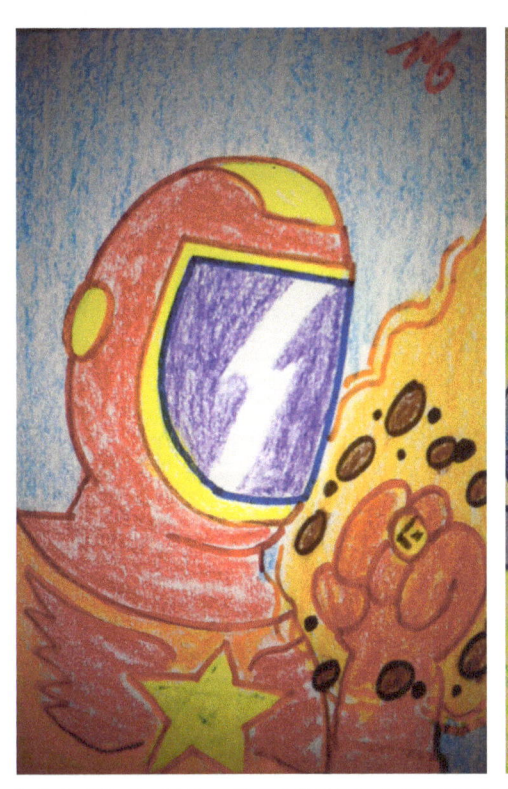
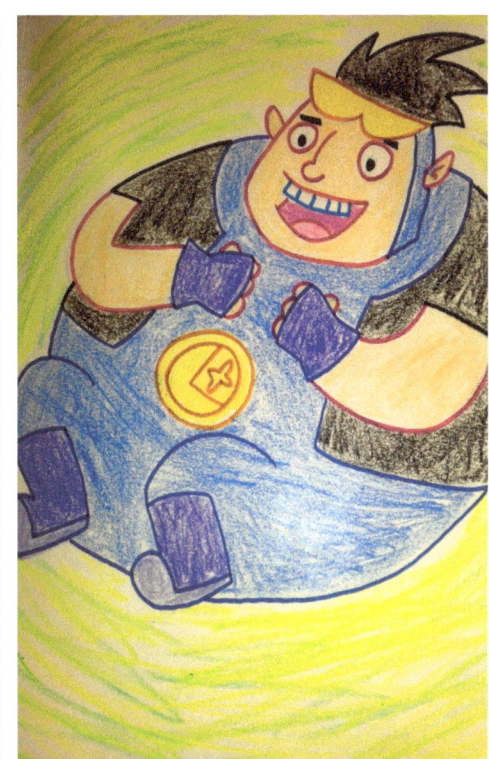
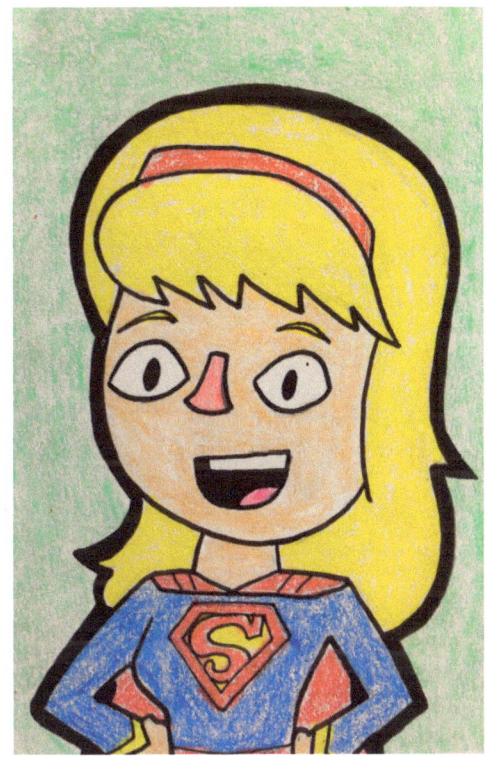
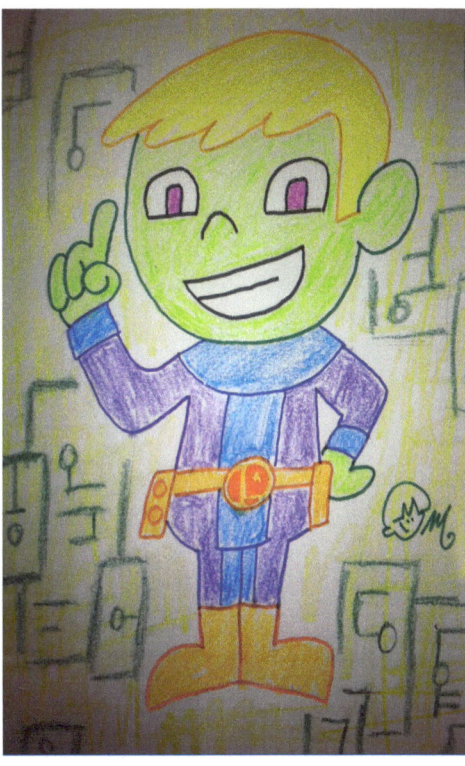

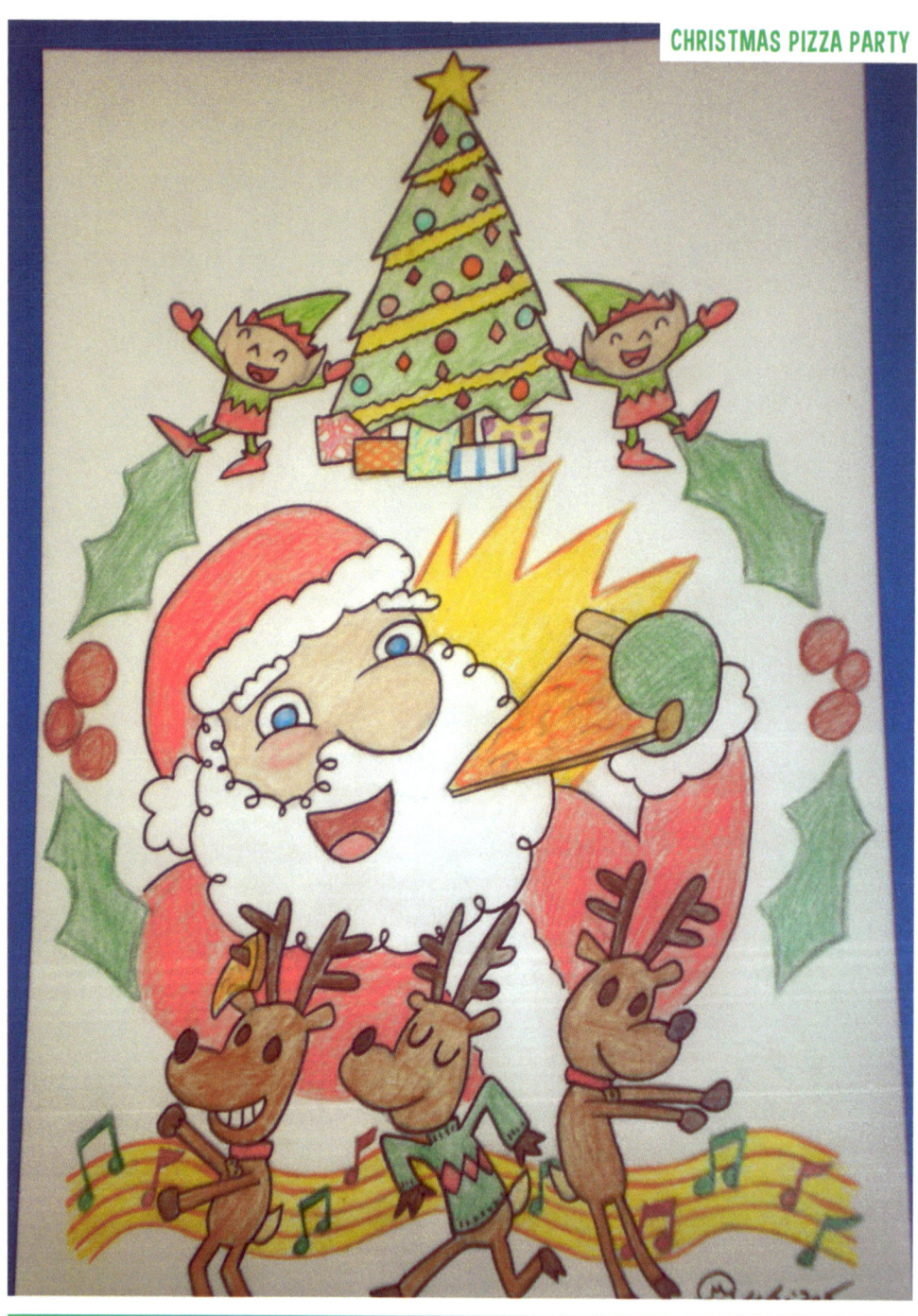